THE COMPLETE
SUPER BOWL
—STORY—

GAMES I–XXVIII

Richard J. Brenner

EAST END PUBLISHING, LTD

To Anita, without whose help I could not have
written this book. Thank you!
To Jason and Halle, as always, with love.

**For details on how to order other exciting sports
books, please see back pages.**

ACKNOWLEDGMENTS

McCoy, Bob, ed. *The Sporting News Super Bowl*. St. Louis,
MO:
The Sporting News, 1986, Edition

Sahadi, Lou. *Super Sundays I–XVI*. Chicago, Illinois:
Contemporary Books

The New York Times, New York.

Cover Photo: Jonathan Daniel, ALLSPORT USA

Library of Congress Catalog Card Number: 87-30328
ISBN: 0-943403-31-6

Library of Congress Cataloging-in-Publication Data

Brenner, Richard J., 1941–
  The Complete Super Bowl Story.

  Summary: Presents, in text and illustrations, highlights of the
twenty-eight Super Bowl games.
  1. Super Bowl Game (Football)—History—Juvenile, literature.
[1. Super Bowl Game (Football)—History]
1. Title.
GV956.2.S8B74 1987   796.332'7   87-30328
ISBN 0-943403-31-6

Printed in the United States of America

**This book is available at special quantity discounts for
bulk purchases for sales promotions, premiums, fund-
raising or educational use.**

**For details write East End Publishing, 54 Alexander
Dr., Syosset, New York 11791, or call 516-364-6383.**

CONTENTS

SUPER BOWL I

January 15, 1967

GREEN BAY vs. KANSAS CITY
"Titletown, U.S.A."

WHEN THE NATIONAL Football League began its 40th season in 1960, it had a new and unwanted rival—the American Football League. At first, the NFL ignored the new league and its eight teams. They reasoned that football fans wouldn't waste their time and money watching NFL rejects in the AFL when they could watch the "real thing."

But each year, the AFL drafted and signed better and better players from the ranks of the college seniors, and football fans soon began to argue over which league had the stronger teams.

The two leagues were paying huge sums of money to unproven rookies as they tried to outbid each other for the most promising college players, but they had agreed not to raid players who were already under contract. That agreement broke down after the 1965 season, however, when the New York Giants of the

NFL signed Pete Gogolak, a field-goal kicker who had been playing with the Buffalo Bills of the AFL.

The owners of the AFL teams decided that the signing of Gogolak was an "act of war" and they appointed Al Davis as their commissioner to strike back at the older league. Davis decided to hit the league where it would do the most damage—the AFL would sign the NFL's top quarterbacks!

The plan worked so well—the AFL quickly signed up seven of the NFL's best quarterbacks—that, within two months, the NFL had cried "uncle" and agreed to a peace plan. The new agreement allowed the NFL to keep the quarterbacks whom the AFL had signed and put a stop to all raiding of players; decided that only one team could draft a college player so that they would stop bidding against each other and not have to pay such large bonuses to rookies; agreed that the two leagues would merge together for the 1970 season; and also agreed that the fans would finally get their wish: There would be a championship game pitting the top AFL team against the top NFL team.

The game would be called the Super Bowl.

The first Super Bowl—cleverly named Super Bowl I —was played on January 15, 1967, in Los Angeles's Memorial Coliseum. The contest matched the Kansas City Chiefs of the AFL against the Green Bay Packers of the NFL.

It was appropriate that those particular teams should be the first participants in football's greatest game. Lamar Hunt, the owner of the Chiefs, had been the person who had had the original idea to form the AFL, and he was the person most responsible for its success. He was also the person who, with a large assist from his children, came up with the idea for calling the game the "Super Bowl."

"My kids had a ball about the size of a handball but it bounced about ten times higher than any normal ball. It's called a Super Ball. My kids talked about it so much that the name stuck in my mind and, when I met with the other owners to discuss the game, the name Super Bowl just popped out of my mouth."

The Chiefs had romped through the regular season with an 11-2-1 record and had won their last 8 games. They had led the AFL in scoring with 448 points (the next closest team only had 358), and in rushing average. Their trio of running backs—rookie Mike Garrett, Curtis McClinton, and Bert Coan,—had ranked among the top nine rushers in the league. Quarterback Len Dawson had led the league in passing accuracy while tossing 26 touchdown passes. Otis Taylor was an excellent wide receiver and tight end Fred Arbanas was one of six Chief offensive players that had made all-AFL.

The Chiefs were also strong on defense with two all-AFL players, big Buck Buchanan (6'7" and 287 pounds) and Jerry Mays, anchoring the line. Bobby Bell at linebacker, and the two safeties, Bobby Hunt and the clever Johnny Robinson, gave the Chiefs *five* all-AFL performers on defense!

The Chiefs were big and fast and well-coached by Hank Stram. Stram was an inventive coach who had devised the "I" formation (where the halfback and fullback line up behind one another instead of alongside each other) as well as the moving pocket, which made it more difficult for the defensive unit to sack the quarterback. Stram was always coming up with new formations and new ideas. His coaching strategy was to show his opponents a lot of different looks and formations that would cause a moment's confusion. "We want to shrink their reaction time," said Coach Stram.

As Joe Collier, the coach of the Buffalo Bills put it, "When you prepare for Kansas City, you work overtime, lots of overtime." They could have used more work, more overtime and better players, though, because the Chiefs had blown away the Bills in the AFL championship game, 31–7.

In 1958, the season before Vince Lombardi became the head coach of the Green Bay Packers, the team had a record of 1-10-1. "Their offense," as one humorous sportswriter noted, "was like a conga dance: 1, 2, 3, and kick."

Before the next season began, Lombardi hired a new coaching staff and they spent hours every day watching films of the Packer games to see which players could help the team become winners. Lombardi also prepared for the college draft and brought in a bunch of new players. He signed "Fuzzy" Thurston, a player who had been dropped by three teams but who eventually went on to become an All-Pro at left guard for Green Bay. He also made a great trade with Cleveland that brought the Packers three players who were destined to become cornerstones of the Packer defense: tackle Henry Jordan and ends Willie Davis and Bill Quinlan.

Lombardi had prepared well, and when training camp opened for the 1959 season, he let the team know exactly how he felt. "Gentlemen," he bellowed, "I have never been on a losing team, and I have no intention of changing now. You're here to play football, and I'm here to see that you do your very best. I want total dedication on the part of every man in this room."

The team responded by winning its last four games and posting a winning record of 7-5. By the following year, "the Pack" was good enough to win the Western

Conference championship, and although they lost the NFL championship to the Eagles, 17-13, they had served notice that they were no longer losers.

The team had learned how to win, though, and when they went on to capture NFL championships in 1961 and 1962, Green Bay began calling itself "Titletown USA." Then they came back and won again in 1965 and 1966. The 1966 championship had been especially rewarding because it allowed them to represent the NFL in Super Bowl I and because they had turned back the challenge of the young Dallas Cowboys when some people had begun to whisper that Green Bay had gotten old. But when the game was on the line and Dallas had a first and goal on the two-yard line, Green Bay had dug in and lassoed the Cowboys by intercepting a Don Meredith pass in the end zone.

This Packer team was not as strong as the 1962 team, which had featured the slashing running of Paul Hornung and Jim Taylor and an unyielding defense; but it still had five All-NFL players on defense and Bart Starr, who had developed into the best quarterback in football. And it was still strong enough to be rated a two-touchdown favorite over Kansas City.

The Chiefs couldn't wait for the game to begin so that they could show that the AFL was just as tough as the NFL. Their quarterback, Len Dawson, who had been a reserve in the NFL for five years, summed it up when he said, "We're really happy to be getting the opportunity to compete against the NFL and show that we are as good as they are. I know that it will be a rough game because Green Bay has a great team. They always believe that they will win and this was evident in their game against Dallas. That goal-line stand showed what the Packers were about."

All the Chiefs, with the exception of corner back Fred Williamson, respected the ability of the Packers. But Williamson, known as "The Hammer" for the way he used his right arm to deliver karate blows to receivers, wasn't impressed with the Packers. "I haven't seen anything in the films that offers much of a threat. The Green Bay receivers don't rate with the top receivers in our league. And Bart Starr, who is he, anyway?"

Coach Lombardi was confident that, if they played their best, his team could beat the Chiefs, but he was concerned that they might not take an AFL team as seriously as they would an NFL team. To stir them up, he appealed to their pride and reminded them that their efforts would reflect on the entire NFL.

Green Bay took the opening kickoff, but after gaining one first down, they were stopped by the hard-charging Chiefs who sacked Starr twice. The Packers struck quickly the next time they had the ball, though, as Starr led them on a six-play, 80-yard drive. The last play of the drive was a 37-yard touchdown pass to wide receiver Max McGee, who had just come in to replace the injured Boyd Dowler. McGee made a sensational one-handed grab, and then outraced Fred "The Hammer" Williamson to score the first touchdown in Super Bowl history. As Max said after the game, "When the ball stuck in my hand, I almost fainted." "The Hammer" wasn't feeling so great, either.

The Chiefs were moving the ball, but all they had to show for their efforts in the first quarter was a missed field-goal attempt. In the second quarter, though, Dawson led the Chiefs on a 66-yard drive and ended it with a 7-yard touchdown pass to fullback Curtis McClinton, and the score was tied, 7-7.

Green Bay took the kickoff and started a typical Packer drive by grinding out 73 yards in 13 plays. Jim Taylor scored the TD with a 14-yard run on the famed Packer sweep as guards Fuzzy Thurston and Jerry Kramer escorted him into the end zone for a 14-7 lead.

But the Chiefs refused to quit and, led by Dawson's 4-for-4 passing, they positioned themselves for a 31-yard Mike Mercer field goal with less than a minute left in the half. Green Bay's lead was cut to 14-10.

Most people were surprised at how close the score was, and at how well the Chiefs were playing. KC had actually outgained the Packers 181 yards to 164 and made 11 first downs to Green Bay's 9. One NFL executive, in fact, predicted that "the Packers will wilt from the heat and their age in the second half."

Lombardi spent a few minutes discussing a strategy change with his assistant coaches. Then he walked into the player area and told the team that they weren't playing hard enough, weren't blocking or tackling with determination. He looked around the room at each player and then he asked the team, "Are you the World Champion Green Bay Packers or aren't you? Get out on that field and answer me."

The Packers stormed onto the field for the second half, determined to dominate the Chiefs and uphold the traditions of Green Bay. The Chiefs took the kickoff and had a third down and 5 at their 49-yard line, but it was then that the Packer strategy and effort put an end to the Chiefs' plans.

Dawson had been getting too much time to pass so the Packers decided to blitz. In fact, the Packers sent both outside linebackers, Dave Robinson and Lee Roy Caffey, blasting into the Kansas City backfield to try to sack Dawson. They didn't quite reach him but they did cause him to hurry his throw. Free safety Willie

Wood stepped in front of the intended receiver, intercepted the hurried toss, and raced all the way down to the Chiefs' five-yard line before he was tackled. One play later, Elijah Pitts carried the ball in to give Green Bay a 21-10 lead—and the rout was on.

The Packers added another score in the third period when Starr hit McGee with a 13-yarder. McGee, who had caught only four passes for 91 yards and one touchdown during the entire season, wound up with seven catches for 138 yards and two scores in the Super Bowl! Pitts closed out the scoring with a 1-yard run in the final quarter to give the Packers a 35-10 victory.

The Packer defense was so superior in the second half that Kansas City was only able to cross midfield once—and only for one play in the entire second half. And Dawson, chased by Packer defenders, could complete only 5 of 12 passes for a measly 59 yards after the intermission.

After the game, talking about the interception, Chiefs' coach Hank Stram said, "That interception was the key play of the game." Dawson agreed. "It gave them the momentum. They took the ball and shoved it down our throats." Jerry Mays, their tough defensive end, added sadly, "We lost our poise. Great teams don't lose their poise." Willie Wood, who made the interception, talked about how Lombardi, during halftime, had chided the players for their sloppy play. "We got the message," said a smiling Wood.

The question as to which league was better had been answered, at least for that year. Lombardi tried to be gracious by saying that the Chiefs were a fine football team with good speed. But in the end, his honesty won out and he added, "In my opinion, the

Chiefs don't rate with the top teams in the NFL. Dallas is better and so are several others."

And what happened to The Hammer? One of the Packers blocked him so hard on one play that he was knocked out of the game!

SUPER BOWL II

January 14, 1968

GREEN BAY vs. OAKLAND
"One More Time"

THE SCENE OF Super Bowl II shifted to Miami's Orange Bowl Stadium but Green Bay was again onstage. After a rocky year, the Pack was back. Before the season had even started, the Packers had lost their long-time starting backfield of Paul Hornung and Jim Taylor. Then their replacements, Elijah Pitts and Jim Grabowski, came down with injuries, and Lombardi had to reach out for two fullbacks, Chuck Mercein and Ben Wilson, who had been discarded by many teams, to pair up with veteran halfback Donnie Anderson and rookie Travis Williams. And Bart Starr, who was not getting any younger, had missed four games because of injuries.

Green Bay had limped to the Central Division crown (1967 was the first year that the Western and Eastern conferences were broken up into divisions) with a 9-4-1 record. They had had to face the Los Angeles Rams for the Western Conference title and the Rams, who had won their division with an 11-1-2 record, had come from behind to beat the Packers, 27-24, just two weeks before in a regular-season game.

LA struck first, but the Packers struck harder. The speedy Travis Williams dashed for two scores on runs of 46 and 2 yards. Chuck Mercein added a 6-yarder and Bart Starr had a hot hand as he went 17 for 23, including a 17-yard score to Carroll Dale. The defense dug in and the Pack went on to trounce the Rams, 28-7.

For the second consecutive year, the Packers had to butt heads with the Dallas Cowboys for the NFL title, and Dallas had just shown how tough they could be by annihilating a solid Cleveland team, 52-14, to gain the Eastern Division crown. The game was a classic struggle that was played in horrible weather. The temperature at game time was 13° below zero and 15-mile-an-hour winds swirled around the frozen earth at Lambeau Field in Green Bay.

Green Bay jumped out to a 14-0 lead on two touchdown passes from Starr to Boyd Dowler, but Dallas cut the lead to 14-10 by half time. After a scoreless third quarter, halfback Dan Reeves threw a 50-yard TD to wide receiver Lance Rentzel with eight seconds gone in the fourth quarter to give Dallas a 17-14 lead. With only a few minutes remaining in the game, the Packers got the ball back for one last chance. From their own 32, they marched down to the shadow of the Dallas goal line. Twice Donnie Anderson was given the ball but he could not get traction on the icy field and was stopped short of the end zone. With 13 seconds and no time-outs left, Starr brought the Packers up to the line of scrimmage for the last play of the game. As the players, steam puffing from their mouths, tensed, Starr called the signals. "Hut, hut," he barked, and then the two lines crashed together. Starr kept the ball himself and, behind a crunching block by right guard Jerry Kramer, dove into the end zone to give the Packers the game and their third straight NFL championship.

After the game, Kramer told reporters how he had looked for and found a toe hold where he could plant his foot and gain the traction that he needed to push back the bigger and heavier Jethro Pugh. "It was," said Jerry, "a lifetime situation and this was the one shining moment."

The great Packer defensive end Willie Davis observed, "I guess a 9-4-1 record isn't great, but we had it when we needed it." But now they would have to do it one more time—in the Super Bowl against the young and talented Oakland Raiders.

The Raiders had raced through their AFL schedule with a 13-1 record (the loss being a 3-pointer against the New York Jets). And then they had gone on to rout the Houston Oilers in the AFL championship, 40-7!

The Oakland offense, which was quarterbacked by Daryle Lamonica, had led the AFL in scoring with 468 points. Lamonica had been obtained in a brilliant trade by Al Davis, the man who runs the Raiders. Daryle, in his first season as a starter after riding the Bills' bench for four years, had gone on to lead the league in passing while tossing 30 TD passes and being named the AFL's MVP! Daryle could throw short or long and he could also run when he had to. In addition to his athletic talent, he quickly became, according to coach Johnny Rauch, "the leader of our team."

Oakland had a strong offensive line that featured two truly great players, guard Gene Upshaw and center Jim Otto; fine wide receivers in Bill Miller and Fred Biletnikoff; and two bruising runners, Pete

Banaszak and Hewritt Dixon. But most people felt that the defense, nicknamed "The 11 Angry Men," was the real strength of the Raider team. The heart of the defense was tackle Tom Keating, and alongside him was big (6'7", 275 lbs.) Ben Davidson at end. Big Ben was a fierce pass rusher who a few weeks earlier had broken Joe Namath's jaw while sacking the Jet quarterback.

Despite Oakland's accomplishments and the fact that most experts agreed that they were a stronger team than the Chiefs had been last year, Green Bay was still favored to win by two touchdowns. Most of the drama surrounding the game centered not on which team would win but on the rumor that Vince Lombardi might retire from coaching after the game.

Lombardi refused to discuss the matter with reporters but a few days before the Super Bowl, he told his players after a practice, "I want to tell you how very proud I am of you. It's been a long season and Sunday may be the last time we are all together. Let's make it a good game, a game we can be proud of."

Green Bay drove into Oakland territory the first time they had the ball, but they had to settle for a Don Chandler field goal. Early in the second quarter, Green Bay once again drove into Oakland territory, but once again the drive fizzled and they had to settle for another Chandler field goal. The Packers were leading 6-0 but they looked sluggish. Maybe it was too much Miami heat when they were used to frostbite in Green Bay.

A little later in the period, the Packers had the ball on their 32-yard line. Starr called a play-action pass play and faked a handoff in the backfield while wide receiver Boyd Dowler headed downfield. The Raider secondary was fooled by the fake and that allowed

Dowler to get behind his man and grab a 62-yard touchdown toss. Now it was the Raiders who were feeling the heat!

The Oakland offense, which had been smothered to this point, finally got moving as Lamonica led them on a 79-yard drive that featured the running of Banaszak and Dixon. Lamonica capped the drive with a 23-yard strike to Bill Miller, which cut Green Bay's lead to 13-7.

The score seemed to fire up the Raider defense and they forced the Packers to punt. Roger Bird called for a fair catch but he fumbled Anderson's twisting, left-footed kick and Green Bay recovered the ball. With time running out in the half, Starr, after missing with two long passes, hit Anderson with a 12-yarder, which set up Chandler's third field goal, and the Packers led at halftime, 16-7.

During the intermission, some Green Bay veterans decided that, despite their nine-point lead, they weren't playing "Packer football." They weren't concentrating or executing their plays properly. The word went out to the rest of the team: "Let's go out and do it right for Coach."

And they did! They went on a drive early in the third quarter that featured a 35-yard pass to Max Mc-Gee and ended with a 2-yard score by Donnie Anderson. The Packers increased their lead to 26-7 when Chandler kicked his fourth field goal. Then they put the game completely out of reach in the fourth quarter when Herb Adderly intercepted a Lamonica pass and took it 60 yards, helped by bone-crushing blocks by Henry Jordan and Ron Kostelnik, to give Green Bay a 33-7 lead. Oakland added a meaningless touchdown to make the final score 33-14.

As the final whistle blew, Jerry Kramer and Forest

Gregg lifted Coach Lombardi on to their shoulders one last time and, as they walked off the field, he smiled down at them and said, "This is the best way to leave a football field."

This wasn't the best of Packer teams and as Lombardi said, "This wasn't our best effort," yet they had still managed to mangle the best team in the AFL. Was the NFL so much better than the AFL that the Super Bowl would just become the "Super Joke"? A lot of people thought so, but one person, Al Davis, saw things differently. "The difference isn't between the leagues; it's between the Packers and everybody else."

SUPER BOWL III

January 12, 1969

NEW YORK vs. BALTIMORE
"Broadway Joe Lights Up Miami"

WHEN THE BALTIMORE Colts arrived in Florida, they were already being billed one of the best football teams of all time. The question wasn't "Will they beat the New York Jets?" but rather "By how much?"

The Colts, 13-1 during the regular season, had beaten the Vikings to capture the Western Conference title and then avenged their earlier loss to Cleveland by crushing them 34-0 to win the NFL championship.

The Colts' season could have been doomed before it began when Johnny Unitas, considered by many football experts to be the greatest quarterback of all time, injured the elbow of his throwing arm. But luckily for the Colts, they had acquired Earl Morrall during the exhibition season. Morrall, who had played for four different teams in a 12-year NFL career, had always been a backup, but he made the most of his opportunity to become a starter and became the Number-One-rated quarterback in the NFL as well as its MVP!

Morrall was the leader of a high-scoring offense (second highest in the NFL with 402 points scored) that was loaded with talent. John Mackey, a superb receiver and fierce blocker, was acknowledged to be the best tight end in football, and wide receivers Willie Richardson and Jimmy Orr were both outstanding. Tom Matte was a fine all-around running back and Jerry Hill was considered to be the best blocking back in football.

The defense, which had given up the fewest points (180) during the season, was just as strong as the offense. Bubba Smith, a giant at 6'7" and 295 pounds, was a great pass rusher; Mike Curtis was one of the best middle linebackers in the league; and the secondary was solid at every position.

When the Jets arrived in Florida, their quarterback, Joe Namath, caused an uproar. A TV news reporter asked him what he thought about Morrall, and Namath, who always spoke his mind, replied, "I can think of five quarterbacks in the AFL that are all better than Morrall."

The Colt players were enraged at Namath for taking what they thought was an unnecessary cheap shot at their teammate. Lou Michaels, the Colts' place kicker (who also happened to be a burly 250-pound defensive tackle) happened to meet Namath at a restaurant. He went up to Joe and angrily said, "You're doing a lot of talking." The cocky quarterback looked him in the eye and said, "There's a lot to talk about. We're going to kick heck out of your team. I'm going to pick it apart."

Later in the week at an awards dinner, Namath told AFL president Milt Woodward and a room full of diners and reporters, "The Jets will win Sunday; I guarantee it!"

Most people laughed at Namath's boastful announcement, but he was full of confidence and he had a way of backing up his boasts. In the AFL championship game against Oakland, for example, Namath had thrown an interception that allowed the Raiders to take the lead in the final quarter. But he came right back throwing, and with three consecutive completions that gobbled up 68 yards in just 55 seconds, he took the Jets in for the winning touchdown.

And there was more to the Jets than Broadway Joe. He had two star receivers in George Sauer and Don Maynard. In the backfield, Matt Snell was a bruising blocker and a punishing runner, and Emerson Boozer was a constant breakaway threat. The offensive line blocked well enough for Namath and opened up enough holes to have allowed the Jets to score 419 points during the regular season.

The Jets, with stars like Jerry Philbin, John Elliott, and Verlon Biggs on the line and Al Atkinson at middle linebacker, had become a strong defensive team. In fact, one famous football critic—none other than Joe Namath—had said, "The reason we've been winning is the defense."

The experts, who had made Baltimore the 18-point favorite, said that the Colts couldn't lose and Namath had said that the Jets would win for sure. But talk doesn't win football games; it was time to settle the argument on the field.

The Jets took the opening kickoff, and on their first two plays, they sent fullback Matt Snell crashing through the line. Before the Jets were forced to punt, safety Rick Volk came up to tackle Snell and the collision was so fierce that Volk had to be helped off the field. The Jets had sent a message to the Colts: "We're coming right at you!"

The Colts launched a long drive on their first possession as Morrall effectively mixed runs with passes. But Baltimore came up empty when Michaels missed a 27-yard field-goal attempt. Later on in the first quarter, Jet receiver George Sauer fumbled deep in Jet territory and the Colts had a first down at the 12-yard line. Morrall tried to throw for a touchdown but Al Atkinson tipped the pass and Randy Beverly made a diving interception in the end zone.

The fired-up Jets had the ball back at their own 20. Behind the blocking of tackle Winston Hill, they sent Snell smashing into the line on four consecutive carries for 26 yards. Namath hit on a short pass to get the Jets into Colt territory and then, on a third-down play, he hit Sauer for 14 yards and a first down. Another pass to Sauer brought the ball to the Colt 23. Then Boozer ran for 2, Namath hit Snell for 12, and Snell added 5 more on a run to the right to move the ball down to the 4. On the next play, Snell ran to the left and behind devastating blocks by Hill and Boozer, barreled into the end zone with Colt linebacker Dennis Gaubatz hanging on his back. For the first time in Super Bowl history, an AFL team had taken the lead!

Baltimore bounced back when Matte ran for 56 yards and gave them a first down at the Jet 16. But once again the Jet defense stiffened, as Johnny Sample intercepted a pass intended for Willie Richardson. The Colts threatened once more in the half when they surprised the Jets with a flea-flicker. Morrall handed off to Matte who took two steps and then turned and pitched the ball back to Morrall. The Jets were trapped and Colt receiver Jimmy Orr was standing all alone at the goal line. Morrall didn't see him, though, and threw instead toward Jerry Hill, but Jim Hudson, the Jets' strong safety, picked it off and the Jets had their third interception and a 7-0 half-time lead.

During the break, Baltimore coach Don Shula tried to rally his troops but on the first play from scrimmage in the third quarter, Matte fumbled and the Jets recovered. Five plays later, Jim Turner kicked a field goal to up the score to 10-0. The very next time the Jets got the ball, Namath hit Sauer with two passes to set up another Turner field goal, which increased their lead to 13-0.

Shula brought in the sore-armed Unitas to see if he could provide a spark for the Colts. He did lead the Colts to a fourth-quarter touchdown after another Turner field goal, but it was too little, too late, and the "couldn't-lose Colts" lost, 16-7. As Joe Namath jogged off the field, he had a big grin on his face and his right index finger in the air to signal that the Jets were Number One—the Super Bowl champs.

In the winning locker room, the Jets offered different reasons for their victory. Snell credited the offensive line while Boozer singled out the defense.

But George Blanda, the old pro of the Raiders, may have put it best when he said, "Namath psyched two teams. He psyched the Jets into believing that they could win, and he psyched the Colts into doubting that they could win."

SUPER BOWL IV

January 11, 1970

KANSAS CITY vs. MINNESOTA
"Lenny the Cool"

THE STAGE FOR Super Bowl IV moved from Miami to New Orleans, but the experts still favored the NFL team, the Minnesota Vikings, over their AFL opponent, the Kansas City Chiefs.

The Vikings had reached the Super Bowl by winning their division with a 12-2 record, and then coming from behind to knock off the Rams 23-20 to win the Western Conference title before beating the Browns 27-7 for the NFL title.

The leader of the Vikes was their rough-and-tumble quarterback, Joe Kapp. Kapp wasn't a pretty passer, but as Chief coach Hank Stram put it, "He wins. That's the most important thing. And he throws on the run as well as any quarterback I've ever seen." And when Joe wasn't throwing on the run, he was running for yardage. Unlike other quarterbacks, he didn't go down when he was about to be tackled, but instead lowered his shoulder and went right at the tackler. He had done that in the NFL championship game against Cleveland linebacker Jim Houston, and after the collision, Houston had to be helped off the field.

Joe didn't let all the attention he received go to his head. When he was voted the most valuable player on the Vikings, for example, he turned down the award, saying, "There is no one most valuable Viking; there are 40 most valuable Vikings."

"People," he told reporters, "put too much responsibility for a team's success on the quarterback when actually the games are won and lost up front in the line."

The Vikes had plenty of strength on the offensive line, led by Pro-Bowlers Mick Tinglehoff at center and Grady Alderman at tackle. Their record-setting defense, which had allowed their opponents an average of only 9 1/2 points a game in a 14-game season, had three Pro-Bowlers on the line: ends Jim Marshall and Carl Eller and tackle Alan Page. That line had been responsible for destroying NFL offenses.

When asked if he would guarantee a Viking victory, Kapp gave a straightforward reply. "I don't think that anybody can guarantee a football game. There are two great football teams in this game. We're going out there to rock and sock with the Chiefs and may the better team win."

The Chiefs had finished second to the Raiders in the AFC West with an 11-3 record, but because of a new system, they were eligible for the play-offs. They eliminated the Eastern Division champion Jets, 13-6, in a hard-fought victory while Oakland was humiliating Houston, 56-7, behind Daryle Lamonica's six touchdown passes. Then the Chiefs, who had lost to Oakland twice during the season, upset the Raiders, 17-7, to gain the AFL title.

The Raiders jumped out to a 7-0 lead and looked as if they might clobber the Chiefs. "Sure, it looked grim," said defensive end Jerry Mays. "In the past, we would have thought, *Is this one of those days?* But we've matured. Now we never question any situation; we just dig in harder."

The other key factors in the game were a ferocious pass rush led by Aaron Brown, which resulted in an injury to Lamonica's throwing hand, and four interceptions and a marvelous pass by Lenny Dawson to wide receiver Otis Taylor that led to the winning touchdown.

Dawson had never received the attention that many other quarterbacks had, but in his eight AFL seasons, he had thrown 182 touchdown passes, the most of any pro quarterback during that time. Lenny had become a quiet team leader by displaying courage and loyalty to his teammates. "When I lost the sight in my eye," said tight end Fred Arbanas, "I needed somebody to throw passes to me to redevelop my depth perception. Lenny worked out with me five days a week for months. He didn't have to do it, but that's the way he is."

The Vikings were a grind-it-out, ball-control type of team that relied on execution and an intimidating defensive front four to win games.

The Chiefs had a more imaginative offense, which made it a hard team to prepare for, and they also had a tough defense, as they had demonstrated against the Jets and Raiders.

The Vikings took the opening kickoff and racked up two first downs before being forced to punt. The

Chiefs took the ball and drove down to the Vikings' 41-yard line. The Vikes held there but Jan Stenerud came in and gave the Chiefs a 3-0 lead with a 48-yard field goal.

The Chiefs mounted another drive late in the first quarter and when it was stopped early in the second quarter, Stenerud came in again and calmly kicked a 32-yarder through the uprights. The Kansas City defense was smothering the Viking offense and, when the Chiefs got the ball back, they again drove into Minnesota territory, and again Stenerud hit a short field goal to give the Chiefs a 9-0 lead.

Charlie West fumbled the ensuing kickoff and the Chiefs recovered deep in Viking territory. Dawson hit Taylor with a pass down to the five, and three plays later, Mike Garrett ran the ball into the end zone to give Kansas City a 16-0 half-time lead. The Vikings were being blown out!

The Chiefs received the second-half kickoff but the Vikings forced them to punt and immediately began their first sustained drive. Kapp got a hot hand and completed three straight passes to get the Vikes down to the four-yard line. Dave Osborn blasted across on the next play and the Vikes had cut their deficit to 16-7. If they could hold the Chiefs and come back to score again, the momentum of the game could shift in their favor.

But the Chiefs quickly killed that dream as Dawson, using an unusual formation and a short count, hit Otis Taylor with a quick pass and Taylor, after breaking two tackles, went all the way for a 46-yard touchdown and a 23-7 lead. Taylor had not only broken tackles, he had also broken the spirit of the Vikings, and they never threatened again.

The defeat for the Vikings was total and even the

"indestructible" Joe Kapp had to be helped from the field after he collided with Aaron Brown. "The Kansas City defensive line looked like a redwood forest," Kapp said. "They took the running game away from us." Coach Bud Grant added, "We played a great football team and they beat us. It's as simple as that."

For the Chiefs, who had lost the first Super Bowl, the victory was sweet. And it was especially sweet for Dawson, who had warmed NFL benches for five years in Pittsburgh and Cleveland before coming to the AFL: He was named the game's Most Valuable Player.

SUPER BOWL V

January 17, 1971

BALTIMORE vs. DALLAS
"The Turnover Bowl"

BEFORE THE SEASON began, the 26 pro football teams
had realigned into one league, the NFL, with two conferences: the National Football Conference (NFC) and
the American Football Conference (AFC). The AFC
was made up of the 10 AFL teams, plus the Baltimore
Colts, the Pittsburgh Steelers, and the Cleveland
Browns, which gave each conference 13 teams. Each
of the conferences was then divided into three divisions. The three divisional winners plus the second-
place team with the best record in the division—called
a "wild card"—would compete for the conference
championships. Then the conference champions
would meet in the Super Bowl.

Baltimore won the AFC East and blanked the Cincinnati Bengals, who had won the Central Division,
17-0. Oakland won the AFC West and then defeated
the Miami Dolphins, the "wild-card" team, 21-14. In
the title game, the rushing of Norm Bulaich and the

passing of 37-year-old Johnny Unitas led the Colts to a 27-17 victory. George Blanda, who came in to relieve Daryle Lamonica, made the game close by completing 17 of 32 passes for 217 yards and two touchdowns. Blanda, at 42 years of age, became the oldest quarterback ever to perform in a championship game.

In the NFC, Dallas won the East and beat Detroit, the wild-card team, on a field goal and a safety, 5-0 (not a very exciting game). San Francisco, who had won the West, upset Minnesota, the Central Division winner, 17-14. In the title game, Dallas won its first conference championship after losing in the play-offs for four consecutive years. The Cowboys beat the 49ers behind the running of rookie sensation Duane Thomas, who rushed for 143 yards and one touchdown. Corner back Mel Renfro intercepted a John Brodie pass, which eventually led to the clinching touchdown by fullback Walt Garrison as Dallas won, 17-10.

For the Colts, going back to Miami provided them with an opportunity to make up for their loss to the Jets two years earlier. For Dallas, there was the opportunity to silence all the wagging tongues who said they couldn't win the important games by going all the way and winning Super Bowl V. In the past five seasons, Dallas had won more games—52 of 68—than any team in pro football, but until this year, they had never won a conference title. Even their own players had begun to wonder. "There was a time," said all-pro corner back Mel Renfro, "when I doubted we could win the big game. I don't now."

The Colts were a well-balanced if unspectacular football team. They played tough defense, ran the ball decently, and relied on a group of quality receivers and an aging quarterback, John Unitas. "I can't throw as far, and I can't run as fast as I used to," Unitas acknowledged, but he usually found a way to win.

The heart of the Dallas team was its defense, which was filled with All-Pros like Bob Lilly at tackle, Lee Roy Jordan at linebacker, and Mel Renfro at corner back. In the last six games, the defense had allowed only one touchdown. Craig Morton was not a great quarterback but Dallas had the finest running game in the league with backs Duane Thomas, Calvin Hill, and Walt Garrison.

The Cowboys took the opening kickoff but couldn't move and had to punt. Baltimore was also forced to punt. Dallas tried again, and again had to punt. When Baltimore got the ball a second time, linebacker Chuck Howley intercepted a Unitas pass, which was to become the first of 11 turnovers that would be committed by the two teams. The Cowboys still couldn't move but their punt was fumbled by Baltimore at their own 9 and the Cowboys managed to score 3 points on a Mike Clark field goal. They added another 3-pointer early in the second quarter but Baltimore caught a break when Unitas fired a pass that was tipped by his receiver, Eddie Hinton, then touched by Dallas corner back Mel Renfro and finally wound up in the arms of a startled John Mackey. The play wound up as a 75-yard touchdown and tied the score at 6-6 as Jim O'Brien's extra-point attempt was blocked.

Dallas took a 13-6 lead when Morton hit Thomas with a six-yard pass, which was set up when Unitas fumbled after being tackled by Lee Roy Jordan. When the Colts got the ball back, Unitas was hit as he was attempting to pass; the pass was intercepted and Unitas was out of the game with a rib injury. His replacement was Earl Morrall, who had been the goat in Super Bowl III.

Baltimore fumbled the second-half kickoff and Dallas worked the ball down to the one-yard line before Duane Thomas returned the favor and fumbled the ball back to Baltimore.

In the fourth quarter, after two more Baltimore turnovers, a Morton pass was deflected and picked off by safety Rick Volk, who ran it back to the three-yard line. Two plays later, Baltimore managed to avoid a fumble or an interception and Tom Nowatzke scored the tying touchdown.

With less than a minute left to play, Craig Morton fired a pass that went through the hands of the intended receiver and was picked off by Mike Curtis who returned it to the Dallas 28. Two plays later, with five seconds showing on the clock, rookie Jim O'Brien kicked a 32-yard field goal and the Colts had won, 16-13. They also got to take possession of the Super Bowl trophy, which had been renamed, the Vince Lombardi Trophy.

The Colts said that the frequent turnovers were caused by punishing defensive hits. "It may have looked sloppy," said safety Jerry Logan, "but it was a great defensive football game."

To most observers, it was merely a colossal comedy of errors committed by a class of circus clowns.

SUPER BOWL VI

January 16, 1972

DALLAS vs. MIAMI

"The Doomsday Defense"

THE MIAMI DOLPHINS, who finished 10-3-1, made it to
New Orleans for Super Bowl VI the hard way—they
earned it. First they won a thrilling 27-24 overtime
victory over the Chiefs in the longest football game
ever played. Garo Yepremian, who kicked the winning field goal 22 minutes and 40 seconds into the
overtime, said happily, "That ball going through the
goalposts is a picture I'll never take out of my mind."
Then they shut out Baltimore, 21-0, as Dick Anderson
intercepted three Johnny Unitas passes and ran one of
them back for a 62-yard touchdown!

Their opponents were the Dallas Cowboys who, after finishing the season at 11-3, beat the Vikings (20-
12) and the 49ers (14-3) without yielding a touchdown

to either team to make it to the Super Bowl for the second consecutive year.

The Dolphins had been a losing team for the first four years of their existence but when Don Shula took over as coach in 1970, they began to win, and two years later, they had made it to the Super Bowl. As their quarterback, Bob Griese, put it, "Our club was ready to go; we were just looking for someone to take us."

The Dolphins, who were the youngest team ever to make it to a Super Bowl, had outstanding talent on offense. Griese had been the top-rated quarterback in the AFC, throwing for 19 touchdowns. Griese was also a strong leader and, as noted by Shula, "Bob has a magnificent football brain." His favorite target was Paul Warfield, an All-Pro wide receiver who had caught 11 touchdown passes during the season. The real strength of their offense, though, was the running game. Their fullback, Larry Csonka, had finished second in the AFC in rushing with 1,051 yards on 195 carries without a single fumble and Jim Kiick had run for 738 yards and fumbled only once. The two of them, who were close friends off the field, were devastating runners and bruising blockers. As Kiick said, "We're two of a kind. We enjoy running over people. We like to hit. I get as much enjoyment throwing a good block for Larry as I do running the ball myself."

On defense, the main man was middle linebacker Nick Buoniconti. The ten-year veteran was the glue that held together a young and inexperienced defense. As Tom Landry noted, "If we are going to run the ball, we're going to have to get someone to block Buoniconti; he is the key to their defense."

The Cowboys had been struggling along with a 4-3 record when Landry decided to turn the quarterbacking job over to Roger Staubach. The Cowboys went on to rope their next nine opponents and Staubach wound up as the leading passer in the NFC, tossing for 15 touchdowns and only four interceptions. Staubach was also a terrific scrambler and had rushed for 343 yards and two TD's. Bob Hayes, who had caught eight TD passes and who was the fastest man in the NFL, was the major receiving threat. Duane Thomas was again their leading rusher with 793 yards, and Calvin Hill and Walt Garrison provided punch at fullback. And their offensive line, led by All-Pro left guard John Niland, was probably the best in the league.

But with all their offensive weapons, it was their defense, the "Doomsday Defense," that dominated opponents. Dallas's defense, which had not given up a touchdown in the last 25 quarters, was manned by an incredible collection of talented, tested veterans like Chuck Howley, Cornell Green, and Cliff Harris. The leader of the pack was defensive tackle and perpetual All-Pro Bob Lilly. As Jim Kiick put it, "Dallas is real tough to run against and the main reason is Bob Lilly. They play great team defense but he's the one who stands out."

Tom Landry summed up the intentions of both teams when he said, "The running game will be the key to the ballgame, assuming that the turnovers are even. They want to run on us. We want to run on them."

The second time the Dolphins had the ball, they took it into Cowboy territory on a 12-yard sweep around right end by Csonka. But on the next play, he committed his first fumble of the season and Chuck Howley recovered. Twelve plays later, Mike Clark kicked a 9-yard field goal to give Dallas a 3-0 lead.

Late in the second quarter, the Cowboys went on an

eight-play, 76-yard drive with slashing runs by Thomas and Hill doing most of the damage. Staubach capped the drive with a 7-yard toss to Lance Alworth for the touchdown and Dallas led, 10-0. Only 75 seconds were left in the half but Griese hit Warfield twice and Kiick once to get close enough for Yepremian to kick a 31-yard field goal and reduce the deficit to 10-3.

Shula was confident that the Dolphins could win. "Our defense had controlled Staubach. He had trouble trying to read the coverage and variations that we were using."

But the Cowboys destroyed Shula's confidence as they took the second-half kickoff and went 71 yards in just eight plays, with Thomas going the last 3 for a touchdown and a 17-3 lead. Miami seemed to have lost their spirit and they failed to make a single first down in the third quarter.

In the fourth quarter, the Cowboys closed out the scoring when Howley intercepted a Griese pass and took off for the end zone. Howley, with no Dolphin near him, tripped at the nine, but three plays later, Staubach hit tight end Mike Ditka for the score and the game, 24-3.

The Cowboys set Super Bowl records with 252 rushing yards and 23 first downs. Roger Staubach, who was named the game's MVP, said, "When we run, everything else opens up. I guess," he added smilingly, "I gave Coach Landry a few gray hairs at the beginning when I didn't see open receivers."

The Dolphins weren't smiling. "I'm very disappointed," said Coach Don Shula. "They completely dominated us." Paul Warfield admitted that they had made mistakes, but then he added optimistically, "But we're capable of coming back next year because we have a good young club."

SUPER BOWL VII

January 14, 1973

MIAMI vs. WASHINGTON
"Great Scott!"

WARFIELD PROVED TO be a prophet: Miami was back in the Super Bowl. And they had come back in magnificent style with an incredible and perfect 16-0 record! They were 14-0 during the regular season, defeated Cleveland 20-14 in one play-off game, and then won the AFC title with an exciting 21-17 victory over the Pittsburgh Steelers.

Griese quarterbacked the team through the first four victories but in the fifth game, he broke his ankle. His replacement was Earl Morrall—the same Earl Morrall who had replaced an injured John Unitas for the Colts in Super Bowl III (when Shula coached Baltimore) and for most of Super Bowl V. Morrall provided a steady hand and, throwing infrequently on a team geared to the run, became the top-rated passer in the conference.

During half time of the AFC title game, with the score tied 7-7, Shula decided that it was time to switch from Morrall back to Griese. Shula decided that Griese would also be the quarterback in the Super Bowl because he thought that the offense hadn't been performing well in the play-offs under Morrall's direction. And Shula was a man with a mission—a mission to capture a Super Bowl victory after experiencing defeats, first as the coach of the Colts and then last year when the Dolphins lost to Dallas.

Morrall, of course, was disappointed, while Griese was elated. He wanted to put the experience of last year's loss to Dallas to good use. "We were," he explained, "too anxious to score first. We thought whoever scored first would win and that took us out of our game plan. And then when Dallas did score first, we really sagged emotionally. This time, we're going out to play 60 minutes and win. Our goal isn't to score first, but to score most."

The Dolphins had proven they could score points by leading the NFL in scoring with 385 points. They did it mostly on the ground and they did it well enough to set an NFL record by rushing for 2,960 yards. Larry Csonka with 1,117 and Eugene "Mercury" Morris with 1,000 became the first two runners from the same team ever to gain 1,000 yards rushing in the same season. And Jim Kiick kicked in his share with 521. If you're going to run, you need blocking, and Miami had one of the finest offensive lines ever assembled, with all-pros like Larry Little, Bob Kuchenberg, and Jim Langer.

While the Miami offense had been piling up the points, the Miami defense—known as "The No-Name

Defense"—had been the stingiest in the NFL, and allowed their opponents the fewest points, 171. They had gotten their nickname last year when Tom Landry had said, "I can't recall the names of the players on the Miami defensive unit." The defense adopted the name with pride and refused the suggestion of taking on a more glamorous name.

Their opponents in Los Angeles were the Washington Redskins, who had won their division with an 11-3 record and then gone on to capture the NFC title by beating Green Bay, 16-3, and Dallas, 26-3.

The Redskins were coached by George Allen, a man who had come to Washington two years earlier determined to build a winning team quickly. He believed that veterans win games, not rookies. So he traded away young players and draft choices for older, more established players. "The future," he declared, "is now." The Redskins quickly became the oldest team in the league and were affectionately called the "Over-the-Hill Gang."

Allen dedicated himself to his players and to winning. As Ron McDole, the 34-year-old defensive end, put it, "I've never seen a guy so dedicated to one thing. Football is his life. I've played for five or six coaches and I've never been so well-prepared." Dole also explained why Allen preferred veteran players. "When I played with Buffalo, we had a lot of good young players. But one week we'd look like Superman and the next week like nothing. There was no consistency. They'd see something just a little bit different from what they'd seen before, and they'd mess it up."

Defense was Allen's specialty and the Redskins yielded the fewest points in the NFC, but they also put a lot of points on the scoreboard. Their quarterback was 34-year-old Billy Kilmer. He didn't have a great arm and he wasn't a very pretty passer, but he was able to throw on the run and, most importantly, he usually found a way to win. Kilmer had a quality receiving corps that was led by All-Pro Charlie Taylor, and he also had Larry Brown, the leading rusher in the conference with 1,216 yards.

"I always try to establish the run," Kilmer explained. "It slows down the pass rushers and stops the linebackers from helping out too much on pass protection." Coach Allen had noted, "Both teams live by the run. The team that makes its running game work will win."

The first two times that each team had the ball, they were forced to punt, due to the dominance of the defense. But the third time the Dolphins got the ball, they struck quickly. Kiick picked up 11 yards in two carries and then Griese connected with Warfield for 14. Csonka bulled ahead for 2 and Morris slashed for 4 to the Redskin 32. On third down, Griese completed a pass to Howard Twilley at the 5, and Twilley took it in for the score. Twilley had put such a great move on the defender, Pat Fischer, that Fischer got completely turned around.

Miami lost another score when a 47-yard pass to Warfield was wiped out by a penalty, and then the defenses asserted themselves again. With the half coming to an end, Kilmer tried to pass the 'Skins into position to score, but Nick Buoniconti made an interception and ran the ball down to the Washington 27 before he was stopped.

Instead of going for the quick strike, Griese was patient and called for two running plays. On third down, he hit tight end Jim Mandich with a pass down to the two-yard line. With 28 seconds left in the half, Griese gave the ball to Kiick, who took it to the one as the clock clicked off the seconds. Kiick got the call a second time and this time he got the ball into the end zone to give Miami a 14-0 lead.

The Redskins came out smoking in the third quarter and drove from their own 30 to the Miami 17 as they crossed midfield for the first time in the contest. The Redskins were knocked back on third down, though, when Manny Fernandez sacked Kilmer. They were forced to go for a field goal, but Curt Knight's kick sailed wide to the right and Washington came up empty.

Later in the third period, Miami mounted a drive that featured a 49-yard romp by Larry Csonka that got the ball down to the 16. The Dolphins moved the ball down to the 5 and were all set to sew up the game, but Brig Owens picked off a Griese pass in the end zone and the Redskins were still breathing.

In the fourth quarter, Washington marched 79 yards down to the Miami 10. But once again they came up empty and Miami came up big as Jake Scott intercepted a Kilmer pass and ran it out to the 'Skins' 48. Miami moved the ball down to the 34 and then brought in Garo Yepremian to try a 42-yard field goal. What happened next is probably the weirdest play in Super Bowl history. The kick was blocked by Bill Brundage, and Yepremian, instead of falling on the ball, attempted to throw a pass. The ball slipped out of his hands and Washington corner back Mike Bass grabbed the ball and raced 49 yards for a touchdown, which cut Miami's lead to 14-7, with one minute and 47 seconds left.

The Redskins had one more chance, but Kilmer threw two incomplete passes plus a swing pass to Larry Brown, which lost four yards, and then, on the last play of the game, was sacked by Bill Stanfill.

The Dolphins had won the Super Bowl and they had done it with an unprecedented 17-0 record. After the game, Kilmer explained, "We tried to run against them, but their defense was so good that we couldn't get anything started." Marv Fleming, a tight end who also played on two Super Bowl winners with Green Bay, summed up the feelings of all the Dolphins when he announced, "This is the greatest team I have ever played on."

SUPER BOWL VIII

January 13, 1974

MIAMI vs. MINNESOTA
"Csonked!"

IN 1973, MIAMI "slipped" to a 12-2 record, but not before they had won their opening game to tie the NFL record of 18 straight victories. In the play-offs, they beat the Bengals, 34-16, and ripped the Raiders, 27-10, behind Csonka's three touchdowns to qualify for the Super Bowl, which was played in Rice Stadium in Houston.

The offense still relied on the running attack and their talented line continued to provide the blocks that opened the holes for Csonka to burst through for five touchdowns and Morris to slash through and around. They did it well enough for Csonka to have his third straight 1,000-yard season and for Morris to add 965 and ten touchdowns.

Griese had kept the defenses honest by throwing for

over 1,400 yards and 17 touchdowns; and the defense —featuring two All-Pro safeties, Jake Scott and Dick Anderson—had once again yielded the fewest points in the NFL. They were truly a super team.

Reporters kept comparing the Dolphins to the best teams in football history. Csonka, for one, wasn't interested. "I'm honestly not worried about whether our team is judged to be the greatest of all time. I don't know about legends or statistics. Being here now and playing in the game is my reward." Defensive tackle Manny Fernandez added, "I just play football. I don't worry about whether we're better than the Packers were. The important thing to me is that we're better than the Vikings on Sunday."

Csonka was asked how he thought people would react if the Dolphins lost. "I hope that people in this country realize that not everyone can be a champion. The stress on winning isn't good. There has to be a place for sportsmanship that is appreciated when it does not result in total victory."

Miami's opponents were the Minnesota Vikings, who also finished the regular season at 12-2. Then they whipped Washington, 27-20, and dumped Dallas, 27-10, to earn the NFC title.

The Viking offense was led by Fran Tarkenton, who had enjoyed one of his best seasons. He had completed over 61 percent of his passes while throwing for 15 touchdowns and only seven interceptions. Tarkenton was also a dangerous scrambler who could throw on the run or bring the ball down and run it himself. "He's a marvel," exclaimed Miami's Nick Buoniconti. "He has a sixth sense that tells him when he's in trouble."

Tarkenton was very confident of himself and his team. "When most teams get into an important game," he noted, "they're so afraid of making mistakes that they don't play as well as they can. Our team isn't afraid to gamble. I'll throw on first down, I'll throw from our end zone, and I can throw deep against a zone defense."

Tarkenton's confidence was helped by having All-Pro offensive tackle Ron Yary up front blocking and rookie running back Chuck Foreman, who rushed for 801 yards and added 37 pass receptions, even though he missed three games with injuries. And the defense, led by All-Pro linemen Alan Page and Carl Eller, had given up fewer points than any team other than Miami.

The Dolphins took the opening kickoff out to their 38-yard line. On their first play from scrimmage, Morris ran right for 4 yards. Csonka crashed up the middle for 2, and then Griese hit Jim Mandich for a 13-yard gain into Viking territory. Csonka bulled his way for 16 yards and then Griese hit Marlin Briscoe with a 6-yard pass. Csonka got the next two calls and moved the ball to the 8, and Morris ran it to the 5. Then Csonka, on the tenth play of the drive, drove into the end zone. Miami led, 7-0, and they had made it seem so easy.

After forcing the Vikings to punt, Miami began another drive that lasted ten plays. And on the tenth play, after seven runs and two completed passes, Jim Kiick took it the last yard and Miami led, 14-0.

At the end of the first quarter, Miami had run 20 plays and gained 118 yards. Minnesota had run six plays and gained 16 yards. The Dolphins had eight first downs and the Vikings, none.

And it never got much better for the Vikes. Yepremian kicked a 28-yard field goal in the second quarter to increase the lead to 17-0, and the Vikings did manage to mount a threat, but they fumbled it away deep in Dolphin territory. The Dolphins added another touchdown the first time they had the ball in the third quarter on a 2-yard run by Csonka, and the defense limited the Vikings to a meaningless score by Tarkenton on a 4-yard run in the fourth quarter.

Miami had won its second consecutive Super Bowl and Csonka, who was named the game's Most Valuable Player, broke the Super Bowl rushing record with 145 yards. In describing what it feels like to run through defenses, Csonka said, "You can hear the noise of the clack of the equipment and you can see their eyes peering at you through their face masks and their hands clawing for you. With good blocking, you know you're getting away from them and even for a few yards, that's a great feeling."

After the game, Tarkenton said with admiration, "They are an excellent football team and they played as near to perfect as you can play."

Carl Eller said, "Miami is the best team I have ever played against, and that includes the Green Bay Packers of 1967 and 1968."

SUPER BOWL IX

January 12, 1975

PITTSBURGH vs. MINNESOTA
"The Greene Machine"

FOR THE FIRST time in four years, Miami was *not* playing in the Super Bowl. Oakland had taken care of that when they dethroned the Dolphins, 28-26, on a sensational touchdown grab by Clarence Davis on a pass from Kenny Stabler with only 26 seconds left in the game.

The Pittsburgh Steelers, who had beaten Buffalo, 32-14, in the preliminary round, dashed the dreams of the Raiders, too, by scoring 21 points, including two touchdown runs by Franco Harris, to defeat the Raiders 24-13.

Minnesota won the NFC Central Division for the sixth time in seven years and then smashed the St. Louis Cardinals, who had won the Eastern Division, 34-10. The Vikings beat the Rams, 14-10, for the NFC title as the Minnesota defense stopped the Rams after they had driven 98 yards down to the Viking 2-yard line!

The Steelers had started the season slowly. Quarterback Terry Bradshaw had sat on the bench as coach Chuck Noll decided to start the season with the strong-armed rookie Joe Gilliam. Because Gilliam threw a lot, Franco Harris didn't get to run much. After three games, he had rushed for only 125 yards, and he was forced to sit out the next two games with an injury.

When Noll finally restored Bradshaw to the starting line-up, Terry seemed to have confidence in himself and his abilities, and, after five years, so did his teammates. He had become a leader. He was in control of himself and the game. He still threw with authority but he didn't try to force his passes. And with Bradshaw back, the Steelers went back to a balanced offense that featured the running game.

The main man in the running game was definitely Franco Harris, who combined the power of a fullback with the speed of a halfback to terrorize opposing defenses.

"I really work at it," Franco pointed out. "I know that a lot of things come naturally to me, but I feel better when I know that I have really worked for something." He had worked hard enough to rack up 881 yards in the Steelers' last nine games to finish with over 1,000 yards for the second time in three years, despite his slow start. Franco's running mate was Rocky Bleier, a hard-working halfback, who was an excellent blocker and who could also run and catch a pass. The two backs ran behind an excellent offensive line—you can't run or pass effectively without solid blocking—that included guards Jim Clack and Sam

Davis, tackles Gordon Granville and John Kolb, center Ray Mansfield, and tight end Larry Brown.

The Steelers' plan on offense was to run at the Vikings. It was what Pittsburgh did best and they had seen how effectively Miami had run against the Vikings in last year's Super Bowl. By limiting the number of passes they threw, the Steelers would also avoid the fierce rush of the Viking defense, which had led the league in quarterback sacks with 52. Alan Page and the rest of the Purple People Eaters—the nickname given to the Viking defense because of their purple jerseys and ferocious play—loved to gobble up quarterbacks and running backs.

The Steelers were strong on offense, but they were *awesome* on defense! They didn't just defend, they *attacked,* and the main attacker was their left tackle, "Mean" Joe Greene. Greene, who had been named the defensive player of the year for the second time in the last three years, had plenty of help. At left end was another All-Pro and a devastating pass rusher, L. C. Greenwood, and on the right side of the line were two stars, Ernie Holmes and Dwight White. The two outside linebackers, Jack Ham and Andy Russell, had both made All-Pro and the middle linebacker was a tough rookie named Jack Lambert. The defensive secondary, which consisted of corner backs Mel Blount and J. T. Thomas and safeties Mike Wagner and Glen Edwards, was swift and smart and hit like hammers.

The Steeler players wanted to win the Super Bowl for all the usual reasons, but they also had an added incentive: They felt a strong affection for the 73-year-old owner of the Steelers, Art Rooney. Rooney had owned the Steelers from their beginning back in 1933, and in all that time—42 years—Pittsburgh had *never* before made it to any championship game. They had finally made it to THE GAME and now they wanted to win it for the man who had waited so long.

Pittsburgh had started down the road to the Super Bowl when they had hired Chuck Noll as coach six years earlier. Dan Rooney, one of Art's sons, who had interviewed Noll for the job, recalled, "I liked his attitude and the way he evaluated our team. Everything he said was right on target." Art Rooney added, "His first year, we won the first game, then we lost the next 13, but he never lost his poise or control of the ballclub. He was always honest."

When the Vikings failed to beat Miami the previous year, they became the *only* team that did not win the Super Bowl after having lost it once. The Vikings had lost two Super Bowls and there is a saying that things happen in groups of three; The Vikings didn't want to hear about it.

The game figured to be low-scoring because each team had such excellent defense (Pittsburgh had given up the fewest points in the AFC (189) and Minnesota had only given up 195 in the NFC). But if the Vikings were going to win, they'd have to find a way to score more than the 7 points they had scored against Miami in Super Bowl VIII.

Most of the Vikings' hopes for scoring were placed on the right arm, quick feet, and fast brain of quarterback Fran Tarkenton. As Joe Greene put it, "We're going to have to find a way to stop him. Whatever he can do to hurt you, he will. He scares me more than any other quarterback we've played against because he's so clever." Greene, by the way, didn't like the nickname "Mean Joe." He had gotten the name earlier in his career, but it didn't stick until one afternoon when Joe had spent most of the game trying to corral the scrambling Tarkenton when Fran played for the

Giants. "I kept chasing him and I didn't get him. When I finally did get a shot at him, I was so frustrated that I didn't realize that he had thrown the ball about five minutes before."

The Steelers were favored to win by most people, including Bud Goode, a sports computer analyst. Goode fed a lot of data into his computer and then came up with a concept of how the game would go. "It should be played between the 20-yard lines. But Pittsburgh will be deep in Minnesota's territory more than Minnesota will be deep in Pittsburgh's territory.

"So Pittsburgh's Roy Gerela will kick some field goals and the Vikings will fall behind. Then Tarkenton will have to go to the long pass and he will be working against the Number-One pass defense in the league. What will that mean? Interceptions.

"And Pittsburgh will also be in position to control the game with their superb ground game."

What does a computer know about football? Goode and his computer picked the winner in each of the six play-off games that season!

The Steelers took the opening kickoff and the Viking defense took charge. After allowing a 3-yard gain by Bleier, Minnesota dropped Harris for a 1-yard loss and Bradshaw for a 4-yard loss. After Pittsburgh punted, Tarkenton hit wide receiver John Gilliam for 16 yards but then the Steeler defense forced a punt.

As expected, the remainder of the first quarter was dominated by the defenses. The Vikings were limited to 20 yards passing, none rushing, and only one first down. The Steelers did a bit better with 15 yards passing, 64 rushing, and four first downs. They even got close enough for Roy Gerela to attempt two field goals, but he missed the first one and the second one never got off the ground because of a bad snap from center.

The Vikes had the ball in Steeler territory for the first time in the game when they recovered a Bleier fumble at the 24. But they could only move 2 yards in three plays and wasted a golden opportunity to score when Fred Cox missed a 39-yard field-goal try.

Later in the period, the Vikes had the ball deep in their own territory at the ten. Tarkenton pitched the ball back to fullback Dave Osborn, but it was poorly thrown and Osborn fumbled it. Tarkenton recovered the ball in the end zone to prevent a Steeler touchdown, but they did record a safety and took a 2-0 lead.

Minnesota finally got untracked late in the first half and drove 55 yards down to the Steeler 20 as Tarkenton smartly mixed his passing with Foreman's running. With only 1:17 left on the clock, Tarkenton hit Gilliam at the 5-yard line, but Glen Edwards made a fierce hit on Gilliam and the ball popped into the air and into the arms of Mel Blount for a Steeler interception. "That play," said Steeler linebacker Jack Ham, "could have made the difference."

Viking ball carrier Bill Brown began the third quarter by taking a solid smash on the kickoff and coughed up the football on the 30-yard line. Franco Harris took it down to the 6 with a 24-yard jaunt around the left side. Then he tried a sweep to the right but the play lost 3 yards, so he tried the left side again and swept in for the game's first touchdown and a 9-0 lead.

The Vikes managed to mount a mild threat later in the period, but it was quickly halted when Joe Greene tipped a Tarkenton pass into the air and came down with the ball for an interception. Greene, who ran the interception back 10 yards to the Vikings' 46, later observed, "I would have liked to go all the way, but I just don't run fast enough."

Early in the fourth quarter, the Vikings created a

break for themselves when they forced Franco Harris to fumble. Free safety Paul Krause recovered on the Steeler 47 and Tarkenton went to work by throwing long to John Gilliam. The pass was incomplete but the Steelers were penalized for pass interference and the Vikes had a first down at the 5. They were only 5 yards away from being back in the ballgame; but they never gained those yards because on the very next play, as Chuck Foreman tried to take it in, Joe Greene knocked the ball out of his hands and fell on it!

The Steelers had the ball, backed up deep in their own territory. After three plays failed to produce a first down, Bobby Walden was brought in to punt. But Matt Blair burst through to block the kick and teammate Terry Brown recovered it in the end zone for a Viking touchdown. Cox missed the extra point but now the Vikes only trailed by 9-6, and there were still more than ten minutes left in the game. If the "Purple People Eaters" could stop the Steelers, the Vikes would have a chance.

But they couldn't stop the Steelers. Pittsburgh went on a classic drive that used up more than seven minutes. The 11-play, 66-yard drive featured six runs by Harris and three clutch third-down completions by Bradshaw. The first one went to tight end Larry Brown and was good for 30 yards. The next one went to Rocky Bleier, who had just run three straight times, and moved the ball to the 5. The last one came as Bradshaw rolled out to his right, which froze free safety Paul Krause for just a split second, and then fired the ball to Brown in the end zone to give Pittsburgh a 16-6 lead. "I thought I had Brown covered," Krause explained. "But then Bradshaw pulled up and Brown got behind me."

The game ended a few minutes later and as Terry

Bradshaw walked off the field, he remembered the hard times at the start of the season, realized how far he and his teammates had traveled. "I just savored the noise and all the emotion. It was just a great satisfying feeling." What made it even better was that the game had been played in New Orleans, and Bradshaw was born and raised in Louisiana.

Franco Harris, who rushed 34 times for 158 yards to break two Super Bowl records that had been set in last year's game by Larry Csonka, was named the game's MVP. Franco believed that Bradshaw deserved a lot of the credit for the victory. "Terry had us all relaxed in the huddle. We had control of the situation except for the time when I fumbled. But when I was coming off the field, Joe Greene told me not to worry about it. 'We'll get it back,' he said. And they did. They did it all afternoon."

The Steeler defense had, indeed, dominated the Vikings. They had shut them out (the Viking score came on a blocked punt) and shut them down as they limited them to only 17 yards rushing and 102 passing. And they did it with two second stringers, linebackers Ed Bradley and Loren Toews, who played most of the second half because of injuries to Andy Russell and Jack Lambert. Coach Noll praised the entire squad, but he singled out the play of Joe Greene. "I've never seen a better defensive tackle, and he is probably the best defensive lineman that I have ever seen."

While the Steelers were celebrating in the locker room, Andy Russell, their defensive captain, presented owner Art Rooney with a game ball. "This one's for the Chief; it's been a long time coming."

Minnesota coach Bud Grant blamed the referees for making what he thought were some bad calls. He suggested that the outcome might have been different if the calls had gone the other way. But Fran Tarkenton saw it differently. "We came to win and we couldn't do it. They were the better team. They deserved to win. They capitalized on their opportunities and we didn't. They were too good for us."

And how accurate did Bud Goode and his computer prove to be? Very. The Steelers won; they had intercepted Tarkenton three times and they had certainly controlled the game with their running attack.

SUPER BOWL X

January 18, 1976

PITTSBURGH vs. DALLAS
"The Challenge"

AT 12-2, THE STEELERS had the best record in the
AFC during the regular season. In the play-offs, they
battered Baltimore, 28-10, and then, in a very hard-
fought game, which was played with snow falling and
a sheet of ice on the field at Three Rivers Stadium,
they ousted Oakland, 16-10, to earn a return ticket to
the Super Bowl.

Franco Harris remained the dominant force in their
offense and he finished as the second-leading ground
gainer in the NFL with 1,246 yards, good for 10 touchdowns. He also caught 23 passes, which were good for
214 yards and another touchdown. Terry Bradshaw
pitched in with a solid season as he threw for 18 touchdowns and only nine interceptions. The Steelers, however, had added an important new dimension to their
starting line-up with the insertions of second-year
wide receivers Lynn Swann and John Stallworth. They
had seen only limited duty the previous season as

rookies, but this year their roles had expanded. Swann had caught 49 passes (11 for touchdowns) during the season. With his great speed, sure hands, and exceptional leaping ability, he had quickly become one of the most respected wide receivers in the league.

The big question, though, was whether Lynn would be able to play in the Super Bowl. He had taken a brutal hit in the Oakland game, which caused him to spend two nights in the hospital with a concussion.

While his teammates worked out during the early part of the week leading up to Super Sunday, Swann sat and watched. A few days before the game, he tried running some pass patterns and catching the ball. Afterward he told reporters, "My timing was off. I dropped a lot of passes. I had to think about my health and whether it would hurt or help the team if I played."

The answer to the question was provided by Cliff Harris. The free safety for the Cowboys, Pittsburgh's opponent in the Super Bowl, told reporters, "Now, I'm not going to intentionally hurt anyone. But getting hit again while he's running a pass route would have to be in the back of Swann's mind. I know it would be in the back of mine."

Swann read what Harris said and got angry and determined. Harris' plan backfired. "He was trying to intimidate me. He said that because I had had a concussion, I would be afraid. Well, he can't scare me or the Pittsburgh Steelers. Sure I think about the possibility of being reinjured. But it's like being thrown off a horse. You have to get up and ride again quickly, or you may be scared for the rest of your life."

On the defensive side, Joe Greene wasn't feeling 100 percent either. He still wasn't fully recovered from an injury to his left arm, which had caused him to miss six games and parts of others. But even with a slightly weakened Greene, the Steeler defensive machine was wound up and ready to ride herd on the Cowboys.

The most wound up player may have been Greene's sidekick at tackle, Ernie Holmes. "I'll be glad to get out of here and into the game," he bellowed. "I'm so mad, I could eat these palm trees." Ernie may have been angry about the unusually bad weather that plagued Miami, or just edgy and ready to go. But the real cause of his anger may have been caused by the fact that he was left off the All-Pro team, while Greene, who had missed almost half the season, was selected.

Dallas, with a 10-4 record, had finished in second place in the NFC East and made it into the play-offs as a wild-card team. They took advantage of their opportunity by beating Minnesota, 17-14, on a last-minute 50-yard pass from Roger Staubach to wide receiver Drew Pearson. Roger had wound up and thrown the ball long and high into a crowd in the end zone and Drew had made a sensational catch. It was a disappointing end to a sensational season for the Vikings. They had gone 12-2 and had gotten great performances from Fran Tarkenton and Chuck Foreman. Fran, who was selected as the NFL's MVP and Offensive Player of the Year, threw for 25 touchdowns and was the top-rated passer in the NFC. Foreman rushed for 1,070 yards and scored 22 touchdowns.

Then Dallas routed the Rams, 37-7, as Staubach threw four touchdown passes—three to halfback Preston Pearson (no relation to wide receiver Drew). Dallas became the first wild-card team to make it to the Super Bowl since the leagues merged.

Staubach was the leader of a powerful attack that

led the NFC in total offense with more than 5,000 yards. Fullback Robert Newhouse was their leading rusher with 930 yards gained. Drew Pearson was the leading receiver with 46 catches and tight end Jean Fugett added 38. Preston Pearson, a veteran who had been cut by the Steelers during the preseason, had been a big player for Dallas. He ran for 591 yards, caught 27 passes for 351 yards, and added 391 yards returning kickoffs. Pearson had been particularly effective in the two play-off games as he caught 12 passes for 200 yards and three touchdowns. Nothing would please Preston more than to increase his totals against the team that had let him go.

On defense, Dallas had a great pass rusher in 6'9" Ed "Too Tall" Jones, a strong linebacking crew, and tough, tight-covering defensive backs.

The coaching staff, led by Tom Landry, had played an important part in helping the team reach the Super Bowl. A lot of the great Cowboy stars of the past, like Bob Lilly, Calvin Hill, and Walt Garrison, were no longer playing. The coaching staff had to integrate 12 rookies into the team, and that took a lot of work and a lot of coaching. The Steelers, by comparison, had only 3 new players on their 43-man squad.

Fran Tarkenton, the quarterback of the Viking team that had lost to Dallas in the play-offs, as well as to Pittsburgh last year in the Super Bowl, thought that the Steelers would win. "Their defense is the most dominating defense I've ever seen. It is also the most frustrating defense I've ever played against.

"The Cowboys," he continued, "have been really hot lately. They played very well against us, and they probably played their best game ever against the Rams. But when it gets to this point in the season, it gets down to defense."

Most experts agreed with Tarkenton, but a lot of them also thought that if the game were close at the end, Staubach could find a way to win it. He had shown a talent for keeping cool and coming up with winning plays in tough situations. Despite Bradshaw's fine performance during the season and in Super Bowl IX, a lot of people still questioned his judgment and ability. They thought that Staubach was more patient and less apt to make mistakes. They pointed to the fact that Staubach had excelled in the play-offs while Bradshaw had thrown five interceptions in the Steelers' two play-off games.

The Cowboys took the opening kickoff and came out passing. Staubach, though, was hit on the very first play by L. C. Greenwood and fumbled. Luckily for them, though, they recovered the fumble. After Dallas punted, the Steelers, as expected, came out running. After gaining one first down, they also were forced to punt, but Bobby Walden fumbled the snap from center and then was downed on the Steeler 29.

Dallas quickly took advantage of the opportunity when Staubach hit Drew Pearson on a crossing pattern for a touchdown. Bradshaw didn't panic and try to tie the game on the long pass. He was patient, stuck to the game plan, and kept the ball on the ground. Four running plays had moved the ball to the 48 before Terry threw his first pass. It was a perfectly thrown 32-yarder to Lynn Swann, who made a marvelous catch and advanced the ball to the 16. Two running plays picked up 9 yards, and the Dallas defense bunched up, looking for the run. Pittsburgh brought in two extra tight ends, which usually signals a running play. But Bradshaw crossed up the Dallas defense by calling for a pass. Randy Crossman, one of the extra tight ends, faked a block to the inside as though it were a running play, but then broke to the outside and caught a perfect Bradshaw pass to even the score at 7-7.

Dallas came right back after the kickoff with a 51-yard drive but the Steelers dug in and stopped it at the 14. So the Cowboys had to settle for a Tony Fritsch field goal and a 10-7 lead.

Later in the period, three Staubach passes helped move Dallas to the Pittsburgh 20. They were in touchdown territory, and a score could force the Steelers out of their game plan and perhaps put the game out of reach. It was at this point that the Steeler defense took over. First Andy Russell dropped Robert Newhouse for a 3-yard loss. Next L. C. Greenwood sacked Staubach for a 12-yard loss, and then Dwight White sacked Roger for a 10-yard loss. Forget touchdown, they were out of field-goal range!

The Steelers got the ball back with only a few minutes left in the half, deep in their own territory. Faced with a third down at their own 10, Bradshaw went deep to Swann, who used perfect timing to leap up and make a sensational tumbling catch at the Dallas 37. The threat stalled at the 19, though, and Roy Gerela missed a 36-yard field-goal attempt.

J. T. Thomas picked off a Staubach pass early in the third quarter and ran it back 35 yards to the Dallas 25. The Steelers couldn't take it in, however, and Gerela's field-goal try sailed wide to the left.

After that second miss, Cowboy safety Cliff Harris walked over to Gerela and said, "Nice going; that really helps us." And then he patted Gerela on each side of his helmet. Jack Lambert, the Steelers' 6'5", 240-pound All-Pro middle linebacker, grabbed Harris and pushed him away. "He was trying to intimidate Roy. We can't have that," Lambert later explained.

Early in the fourth quarter, the Steelers still trailed, 10-7, as Mitch Hoopes, the Dallas punter, waited for the snap at his own goal line. As Hoopes stepped up to kick, reserve running back Reggie Harrison broke through the middle of the line and blocked the ball. It went through the end zone for a safety and cut Dallas' lead to 10-9.

After a safety, the team that is scored on has to kick it back to the team that scored. The Steelers took advantage of this opportunity to move the ball down into field-goal range and this time Gerela came through with a 36-yarder to give Pittsburgh its first lead, 12-10.

Staubach tried to rally Dallas after the kickoff, but his first-down pass was picked off by safety Mike Wagner and returned to the Cowboys 7. The Steelers couldn't cross the goal line but Gerela came through with an 18-yarder and the Steelers led, 15-10, with less than seven minutes left to play.

Dallas couldn't make a first down so the Steelers got the ball back. Their lead was only five points, so they needed either a score or a long drive to run out the clock. They didn't want Staubach and company to have the ball with the game on the line.

The Steelers were faced with a third and 6 on their own 36. Dallas went in to a short-pass defense, thinking that the Steelers would go for a safe call. Bradshaw, though, was thinking touchdown. In the huddle, Terry called on Swann to run a deep post pattern. As the ball was snapped, D. D. Lewis blitzed from his linebacker position. As Swann raced down the field preparing to make his cut across the middle, Bradshaw managed to duck under the hard-charging Lewis. Terry came up with his arm cocked to throw and got the pass off just before he was wiped out by Cliff Harris, who had blitzed in right behind Lewis. So he didn't get to see Swann make a sensational catch at the 5 and glide into the end zone to complete a picture-perfect 64-yard touchdown play. Bradshaw was knocked woozy and left the game with a head injury. In fact, he didn't know that he had thrown a touchdown until later in the locker room. Even then he said, "I'm still a little hazy. I could hear bells ringing." The extra point was missed but the Steelers led, 21-10.

With time slipping through their fingers like sand, Staubach tried to bring Dallas back. He hit Ron Howard to cut their deficit to 21-17. The Cowboy defense forced the Steelers to punt and Roger had one more chance. He moved the Cowboys to the Steeler 38 and threw two incompletions. There was time for one more play, and Staubach took the opportunity to pass into the end zone but safety Glen Edwards intercepted the throw and ran it out to the 33. The game was over. Pittsburgh had repeated as Super Bowl champions.

Bradshaw hadn't panicked; he had passed the test. And Lynn Swann, whose sensational catches earned him the game's MVP award, had answered Cliff Harris' challenge. In the winning locker room, Joe Greene, who had been forced to sit out the second half with an injury, pointed at Jack Lambert and said, "He's the fellow who held us together when things weren't going good. He made the licks that got us going."

Mike Wagner had praise for the Dallas effort. "They play an interesting game. They gave us a good run for our money today."

In the other locker room, Roger Staubach, who had been intercepted three times and sacked seven times (a new Super Bowl record) put it very simply. "Pittsburgh is the best."

SUPER BOWL XI

January 9, 1977

OAKLAND vs. MINNESOTA
"The Big One"

THE VIKINGS WON the NFC Central Division for the eighth time in the last nine years with an 11-2-1 record. In the play-offs, they whipped Washington, 35-20, and then defeated Los Angeles, 24-13, to earn their fourth ticket to the Super Bowl.

The Viking offense once again had been led by Fran Tarkenton and Chuck Foreman. Tarkenton, who already held the NFL career records for completions (3,186), yardage (41,802), and touchdowns (308), had had a fine season. He was the third-rated passer in the NFC and threw 17 touchdown passes with only 8 interceptions, while gaining 2,961 yards. Foreman, who Tarkenton thought was the most valuable player in the entire league, had rushed for 1,155 yards (fourth-best in the NFC), caught 55 passes (second-best in the NFC), and scored 14 touchdowns.

The Vikings had added to the explosiveness of their attack with the addition of two quality wide receivers, veteran Ahmad Rashad and rookie Sammy White. Their talent and speed had accounted for very impressive statistics: Rashad caught 53 passes (fifth-best in the NFC), while White snared 51 (sixth-best). White's yardage (906) and touchdowns caught (10) were both tops in the conference.

Washington Redskin coach George Allen said, "This is the best Viking team I've seen since I've been in the league." Tarkenton thought that it was the best team on which he had ever played, and now he desperately wanted to crown Minnesota's efforts with a victory, finally, in the Super Bowl. "This team," he declared, "has an obsession to win it. It started after last year's play-off loss to Dallas. This team is on fire to play the game."

Perhaps, though, Tarkenton wasn't speaking for every player. Alan Page, a great All-Pro, looked at it differently. "Every week you do your best, and if it's good enough, you win. If it's not good enough, you lose. It's a football game. To win will be nice but to lose will not be the end of the world."

The Oakland Raiders won the AFC Western Division for the seventh time since John Madden had become coach eight seasons before, with a 13-1 record. In the play-offs they nipped New England, 24-21, to avenge their only loss of the season (a 48-17 drubbing in the fourth week of the season). Then they stomped the Steelers, 24-7, for the AFC title to reverse the outcome of the two previous seasons.

The Raiders were led by quarterback Kenny Stabler, who had been rated the top passer in the AFC.

Stabler had compiled a completion percentage of 66.7, the second-highest ever in NFL history, while throwing for 27 touchdowns. "I'm not a real hard thrower like Terry Bradshaw. My game is accuracy, touch, and anticipation."

And Stabler had great targets. Dave Casper, the tight end, was the fourth-leading receiver in the conference with 53 catches, including 10 for touchdowns. Cliff Branch, a wide receiver with great speed, had 46 catches, including 12 for touchdowns. Cliff's receiving yardage was 1,111, which gave him an eye-popping average gain of 24.2 yards per catch! The other wide receiver was Fred Biletnikoff, who had made 32 catches, with 7 of them going for touchdowns.

"We've shown," said Stabler, "that we don't have to establish the running game before we pass. We can pass anytime we want to as long as we have good protection." And as George Allen pointed out, "Stabler gets the best protection in the league. He has time to find the open man and his receivers have the speed and knowledge to get open."

The major sources of this protection were two huge, talented All-Pro performers, left tackle Art Shell and left guard Gene Upshaw. "We're not a fancy team," said Stabler. "We just line up and try to knock you out of there. Nobody's better at it than those two guys." They also opened most of the holes through which the Raider running backs romped. The two best Raider runners were fullback Mark van Eeghen, who had gained, 1,012 yards (fifth-best in the AFC), and halfback Clarence Davis, who had shown breakaway speed while gaining 516 yards.

The defensive line had been hit by injuries early in the season, which caused Madden to shift from a four-man rush to a three-man rush with four linebackers.

They had learned the system and had the talent to put it to use: Players like end Otis Sistrunk and outside linebackers Phil Villapiano and Ted "Stork" Hendricks. They also had a very hard-hitting and aggressive secondary led by safeties Jack Tatum and George Atkinson, and the great Willie Brown at corner back.

Some people thought that the defenders, especially Atkinson, were overly aggressive, after an Atkinson hit had caused Lynn Swann to suffer another concussion in the first game of the season. Steeler coach Chuck Noll had spoken about a "criminal element." Atkinson had added to his reputation when he broke the nose of Russ Francis, New England's huge tight end, during the AFC play-offs.

Atkinson claimed, "I'm not out to hurt anybody. I don't play angry. I play a controlled game. Remember, I'm only six feet and 185 pounds; they're mostly bigger than I am.

"I'm going to hit the other man and he's going to hit me and we both know it. That's the game. If somebody gets injured, that's an accident."

Like the Vikings, the Raiders had a reputation of not winning the big games. They had lost Super Bowl II to Green Bay. And in Madden's eight seasons, they had posted the best record in the league, 83-22-7, but they had lost 6 times in the play-offs, including five AFC title games. They had finally made it back to the Super Bowl and they didn't want the trip to be for nothing.

One thing was for sure—one of these teams would finally shed its image of not winning the big game. And they would get to do it in the Rose Bowl in Pasadena, California. It would be the first time that a professional game had ever been played in the most famous college stadium in the country.

The Raiders had the ball first and, with the help of a

25-yard pass to Casper and a 20-yard run around left end by Davis, moved to the Viking 12. But the Minnesota defense held and Errol Mann missed a field goal from the 29.

The third time the Raiders had the ball, they were forced to punt. But before they could get it off, Viking linebacker Fred McNeill broke through, blocked Ray Guy's kick, and recovered it on the Oakland three-yard line! The Vikes gained a yard to the two, and then gave the ball to Brent McClanahan to punch over. But as linebacker Phil Villapiano tackled McClanahan, he hit the ball with his helmet. The ball bounced free and linebacker Willie Hall recovered it for Oakland.

From there, the Raiders moved 90 yards in 12 plays with Clarence Davis again supplying a big play with a 35-yard run to the left side again. The Raiders, though, were halted at the 7, and had to settle for an Errol Mann field goal.

When Stabler came off the field, Madden, who thought that the Raiders should have been winning 14-0 instead of only 3-0, was screaming. Stabler told him, "Don't worry, Coach, we'll get a lot more."

The next time Oakland got the ball, they did get more points. They moved 64 yards in ten plays, finished off by a 1-yard toss to Dave Casper, and now led, 10-0.

The Raiders got the ball and great field position when Neal Colzie returned the next Viking punt 25 yards to the Minnesota 35. Three running plays and a 17-yard pass to Biletnikoff moved the ball to the 1, and reserve running back Pete Banaszak took it the last yard. The extra point was missed.

In the third quarter, Mann increased the Raiders' lead to 19-0 with another field goal. Then Tarkenton, assisted by two penalties against Oakland, moved the

Vikes 68 yards, capped by a touchdown toss to Sammy White.

Early in the fourth quarter, Tarkenton again had the Vikings deep in Oakland territory, but Willie Hall intercepted a pass to kill the drive. A short four-play drive followed that featured a 48-yard pass play to Biletnikoff, and ended with a 2-yard touchdown run by Banaszak. Oakland had increased its lead to 26-7. Two minutes later, Willie Brown intercepted a Tarkenton pass and galloped 75 yards for another Oakland touchdown. Mann missed the extra point but the Raiders led, 32-7. Minnesota added a second touchdown late in the game but, by that time, the only question in doubt was who would win the MVP award.

Biletnikoff won it with four catches, beating out Casper who also had four and a touchdown, as well as Stabler and Clarence Davis, who had run for 137 yards.

After the game, Tarkenton put it very simply. "They totally dominated us." In the other locker room, a happy John Madden said to his team, "You had a great season. You did a great job. They can't say any more that we don't win the big one."

SUPER BOWL XII

January 15, 1978

DALLAS vs. DENVER
"The End of the Dream"

DALLAS, WITH A 12-2 record, won the NFC Eastern Division. And then, to no one's great surprise, they crushed Chicago, 37-7, and mauled Minnesota, 23-6. Those victories earned the Cowboys entrance to the first indoor Super Bowl—in the New Orleans Superdome.

Roger Staubach had enjoyed another fine season while quarterbacking Dallas to its second Super Bowl appearance in three years. Rookie sensation Tony Dorsett was their leading rusher with 1,007 yards and 12 touchdowns, and their second-leading receiver with 29 catches and 1 more touchdown. And Dorsett, the NFL Rookie of the Year, didn't even become a starter until the tenth game of the season! Preston Pearson, the regular whom Dorsett replaced, had 46 grabs and added 341 yards on the ground. And fullback Robert Newhouse added another 721 yards rushing.

Staubach had a fine complement of receivers, led by Drew Pearson, with a team-leading 48 receptions; Butch Johnson and Golden Richards at wide receiver; and the rugged and sure-handed Billy Joe Dupre at tight end.

The devastating Dallas Doomsday Defense was led by Harvey Martin (the 6'5", 250 lb. right end), who recorded 23 sacks during the season. At the other end was Ed "Too Tall" Jones, and at tackle were Jethro Pugh and Randy White, one of the great linemen of all time. Their linebackers—Tom Henderson, D. D. Lewis, and Bob Breunig—were tough against the run and pass. And their secondary, especially Cliff Harris and Charlie Waters at the two safety positions, was excellent.

The Denver Broncos, 12-2, were the surprise winners of the AFC Western Division over the Oakland Raiders. They stunned the Steelers in the first play-off game and then overcame Oakland, who had entered the play-offs as the wild-card team, 20-17, to qualify for their first Super Bowl.

Denver's offense could be described as capable. Their quarterback was Craig Morton, who had played for Dallas for ten years and had been displaced by Roger Staubach. Morton performed steadily and directed an offense that scored often enough to win.

Denver's leading receiver was Riley Odoms, an outstanding tight end who had the ability to go deep. Their best wide receiver was Haven Moses, who snared 27 passes. They had three running backs who carried the ball about equally. One of them, Otis Armstrong, had been the leading rusher in the NFL in

1974, and could pose difficulties for Dallas. The offense's chief strength was that they didn't make a lot of mistakes. They didn't fumble too often or throw many interceptions. They didn't beat themselves with careless errors.

The backbone of the Broncos was its defense. They played a 3-4 defense that worked well for them because they had four quality linebackers. They loved to blitz and had excellent speed, which allowed them to plug up the holes on running plays and help the backs on passes. The best players were end Lyle Alzado, linebackers Randy Gradishar and Tom Jackson, and corner back Louie Wright.

Denver coach Red Miller was asked how he felt about being the underdog. "On paper, the Cowboys are better, but we've faced that situation all year. There were a lot of teams better overall than we were. What usually happened was that we outplayed those teams and beat them."

On the opening play from scrimmage, the Cowboys tried to surprise the Broncos by running a double reverse. However, Butch Johnson fumbled the ball, but luckily for Dallas, he also recovered it. Dallas wound up punting to the Broncos. After a short drive Denver punted back to Dallas and return man Tony Hill dropped the ball at his 1-yard line but managed to fall on it. A short time later, Tony Dorsett fumbled on the Dallas 19, but Cowboy center John Fitzgerald made the recovery. Three times, Dallas had flirted with danger and escaped.

Denver wasn't able to develop much offense because of the constant pressure of the Dallas defense. And that pressure produced a turnover when Harvey Martin and Randy White hurried Morton into making a poor pass that Randy Hughes picked off at the Bronco 25.

Staubach came in and hit DuPree for 12 yards and then handed off to Newhouse for 3. Dorsett covered the final 10 yards in three plays and Dallas led, 7-0.

On Denver's next possession, Bob Breunig tipped a Morton pass into the hands of corner back Aaron Kyle, who ran it back to the Denver 35. Six plays later, Efren Herrera kicked a field goal and Dallas led, 10-0.

In the second quarter, the first of two key calls that went against Denver occurred. Staubach had a pass intercepted in the Denver end zone but an official ruled that Roger had stepped out of bounds before the pass was thrown. Herrera then cashed in the opportunity by drilling a 43-yard field goal to up the lead to 13-0.

Before the half ended, Denver lost three fumbles and Morton threw two more interceptions. In an entire 14-game season, Morton had thrown only eight interceptions, but in the Super Bowl, he had thrown four in only one half! It was a pathetic performance by Morton and the offensive line, which could not contain the Cowboy rush. The team that never beat itself was self-destructing.

After taking the second-half kickoff, Denver managed to edge into Dallas territory after the Cowboys committed a penalty on a fourth-down play. Jim Turner converted the opportunity by kicking a 47-yard field goal to put Denver on the scoreboard.

Later in the period, Dallas drove to the Denver 45. Coach Tom Landry sent in a play that Butch Johnson relayed to Staubach. "Butch," Staubach said, "run a post."

"But I'm supposed to run an inside route on the play that Coach called," protested Johnson.

"Run a post," Roger ordered.

Butch ran the post pattern and made an incredible fingertip catch while falling into the end zone. He dropped the ball when he hit the ground but the official ruled that he had scored *before* the fumble, and Dallas led, 20-3.

Denver struck back quickly when Rick Upchurch set a Super Bowl record by returning the kickoff 67 yards to the Dallas 26. After Morton just missed having a fifth pass intercepted, he was replaced by Norris Weese. Four plays later, Rob Lytle crashed over from the 1, and Denver only trailed by a touchdown and a field goal, 20-10. Denver had been a strong fourth-quarter team all season and there was still plenty of time left.

In the middle of the fourth quarter of this game, however, Weese fumbled and Aaron Kyle recovered on the Denver 29. On the first play after the fumble, Staubach took the snap and pitched out to Robert Newhouse. Newhouse ran to his left as though it were a sweep, but then he stopped suddenly and heaved a wobbly pass that settled in the arms of Golden Richards for a 29-yard touchdown. Dallas had a commanding 27-10 lead. There would be no fourth-quarter comebacks today; the Denver dream had ended in defeat.

But the Broncos had had a wonderful season while providing their fans with a lot of unexpected thrills. As Craig Morton said, "I'm disappointed but I'm pleased to have been here. We've come such a long way. I can't base my season on just one game."

SUPER BOWL XIII

January 21, 1979

PITTSBURGH vs. DALLAS
"This is Fun!"

THE NFL CHANGED its schedule to 16 games, and the Dallas Cowboys, with a 12-4 record, won their division —as usual. In the play-offs, they axed the Atlanta Falcons, 27-0, and then shut out the Los Angeles Rams, 28-0.

The defending champions had started off slowly but finished with a rush by winning their last six regular-season games. The team seemed to be stronger than ever. Staubach had been the top-rated passer in the league and Dorsett had run for more than 1,300 yards. Tony Hill had come on strongly at wide receiver with 46 catches and Drew Pearson had grabbed 44. The Doomsday Defense was still intact, and was the best unit in the NFL at stopping the run.

The Steelers, 14-2, had the best record in the NFL.

In the play-offs, they dumped Denver, 33-10, and then hammered Houston, 34-5, to earn a return visit to the Orange Bowl in Miami against the team they had defeated there in Super Bowl X.

Most people thought that this was the best Steeler team ever. Bradshaw had had his best season as he threw for 28 touchdowns and passed for almost 3,000 yards. Swann, with 61 catches for 11 touchdowns, and John Stallworth, with 41 catches for 9 touchdowns, were even more awesome than in past years. And Randy Grossman, filling in at tight end for the injured Bennie Cunningham, had helped out with 37 grabs.

The offensive line gave Bradshaw plenty of time to pass and still opened holes for Franco Harris (1,082 yards) and Rocky Bleier (633 yards).

The defense had a few new starters—such as Steve Furness at left tackle and John Banaszak at right end—but there was no change in its ability, and opponents still found it difficult to pierce the famed "Steel Curtain."

Before the NFC championship game, Cowboy linebacker Thomas "Hollywood" Henderson had said that the Rams "had no class" and that the Doomsday Defense would shut them out. He proved to be a prophet with talent as Dallas *did* shut out the Rams. Henderson helped by intercepting a pass and running it back 68 yards for a touchdown, after which he slam-dunked it over the goal posts.

As the Super Bowl approached, Henderson began talking about the Steelers. He predicted another shutout and had some unfriendly things to say about a number of the Pittsburgh players. He put down the talent of Randy Grossman and the intelligence of Terry Bradshaw. "Bradshaw," he said, "couldn't spell *cat* if you gave him the *c* and the *a*."

But Bradshaw wasn't going to be bullied by Henderson's mouth. He was loose and feeling good. "It's already been a great season and this is just dessert. I'm here to have fun. I enjoy the challenge of the game. I'm having a ball and I'm prepared and relaxed."

Joe Greene couldn't be provoked either. "There's always a lot of talk from Texas about how good they are. Our team is just as good, but we take a different approach. We don't say we're the best; we just go out and do what's necessary to get the job done."

Dallas took the opening kickoff and put Dorsett to work. He went left for 9, hit the middle for 16, and then swept to the right for 13. Then Landry decided that it was time for a little deception so he called for a double reverse play. A handoff was fumbled, though, and the Steelers recovered.

After Franco Harris had been stopped twice, Bradshaw came through with a 12-yard pass to John Stallworth. Next he came through with another to Grossman for 10 yards down to the 28. And then he hit Stallworth in the left corner of the end zone to give Pittsburgh a 7-0 lead.

The Cowboys took the kickoff and again set out for the Steeler goal line. But they only got as far as the Steeler 39, and then Staubach was sacked twice for losses: first by Steve Furness for 12, and then by Dwight White for 10, as the Steel Curtain pushed the Cowboys back to their own 39!

Bradshaw continued on his roll when Pittsburgh got the ball back as he hit Harris over the middle for 22 and Swann on the right sideline for 13. The roll was brought to a halt by D. D. Lewis, though, as he stepped in front of Stallworth to make an interception.

Near the end of the quarter, Harvey Martin caused a fumble when he sacked Bradshaw. "Too Tall" Jones pounced on the ball and the Cowboys went to work. Staubach, operating out of the shotgun formation, hit Tony Hill at the 26, and then Tony turned on the afterburners and took it in for the tying score on the last play of the first quarter—the only first-quarter TD scored against Pittsburgh that year.

On Pittsburgh's next possession, Bradshaw went back to pass as Dallas sent two linebackers crashing in on a double blitz. Henderson hit him before he could throw, knocking the ball loose, and Mike Hegman scooped up the loose ball and raced 37 yards for a touchdown and a 14-7 lead. If the Super Bowl were Bradshaw's dessert, he must have been suffering from indigestion!

Bradshaw didn't cave in, though, and on the next series, he looked downfield for Lynn Swann. Swann had run a deep post pattern and was well-covered. So Terry looked for a secondary receiver and found Stallworth all alone on the Steeler 35. Big John took the pass, broke a tackle by Aaron Kyle, outraced the other Dallas defenders, and turned a simple 10-yard pass into a 75-yard score that tied the game at 14-14.

With a few minutes left in the half, Staubach began another drive. In five plays, Dallas moved from their 34 to the Steeler 32. Trying to recapture the lead before intermission, Staubach fired a pass toward Drew Pearson. But Mel Blount picked it off and ran it back to the 29.

As the time ticked away, Bradshaw hit Swann at the right sideline for a 29-yard gain, and then again for 21 yards. With 40 seconds left, Bradshaw fired incomplete. Then, knowing Dallas would be expecting a pass, Terry handed off to Franco, who gained 9 yards, to the 7. It was third-and-1 as Bradshaw took the snap and rolled right. If the Dallas defense laid back, he would try to run it in himself, and if they came after him, he would look for an open receiver. Dallas came up to play the run and Terry stopped and looked into the end zone. He spotted Rocky Bleier and, over the outstretched hands of the charging linemen, Terry lofted a high pass, which Rocky jumped for and caught! The Steelers had retaken the lead, 21-14, with 26 seconds left in the half.

Early in the third quarter after a flea-flicker failed, Dallas drove to the Steeler 10-yard line, mostly on the runs of Dorsett. On third down, Staubach spotted reserve tight end Jackie Smith all alone in the end zone. Although the pass was a little weak, it was catchable. But Smith stumbled and failed to make the catch, and Dallas had to settle for a 27-yard field goal by Rafael Septien.

Early in the fourth quarter, the Steelers faced a third and long, deep in their own territory but Bradshaw got them out of the hole with a 10-yard pass to Randy Grossman. Then he hit Swann, who had dropped the last two passes thrown to him, for 13. After a 5-yard pickup by Harris, a penalty was called on Benny Barnes for pass interference against Swann, and Pittsburgh had a first down on the Cowboy 23. Two plays and a penalty later, the Steelers had a third-and-9 at the 22. Bradshaw guessed that Dallas would blitz, so he handed off to Harris, and Franco ran right by the charging Dallas defense and into the end zone to give Pittsburgh a 28-17 lead.

Dallas fumbled the kickoff and Pittsburgh recovered at the Cowboy 18. Bradshaw threw long for Swann at the back of the end zone. It looked as if the pass were overthrown but Lynn leaped and stretched out as far as he could and caught the ball on his fingertips. Gerela's extra point gave the Steelers a 35-17 lead

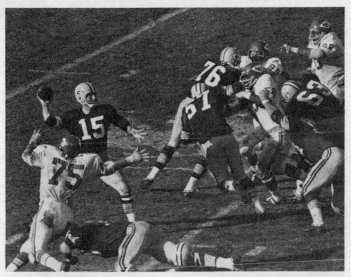

SUPER BOWL I—Starr passes—

SUPER BOWL I—McGee catches . . .
touchdown!

SUPER BOWL III—Joe Namath calls the signals as he checks out the defense.

UPI/BETTMAN NEWSPHOTOS

SUPER BOWL VII—Jake Scott goes high to intercept a pass aimed at Charley Taylor.

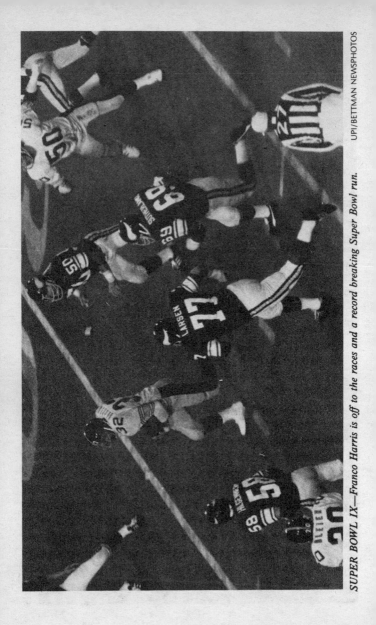

SUPER BOWL IX—Franco Harris is off to the races and a record breaking Super Bowl run.

SUPER BOWL X—Lynn Swann makes an incredible catch while Mark Washington takes a "rest".

SUPER BOWL XIV—Stallworth takes off for the end zone.

SUPER BOWL XVI—MVP Joe Montana is a happy man as he clutches the Vince Lombardi trophy.

SUPER BOWL XVII—*John Riggins breaks away from Don McNeal for touchdown.*

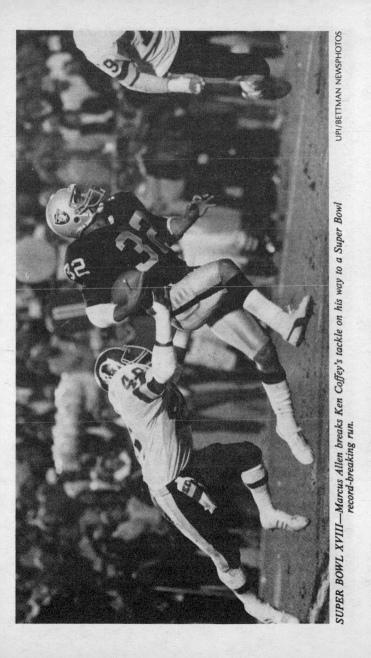

SUPER BOWL XVIII—Marcus Allen breaks Ken Coffey's tackle on his way to a Super Bowl record-breaking run.

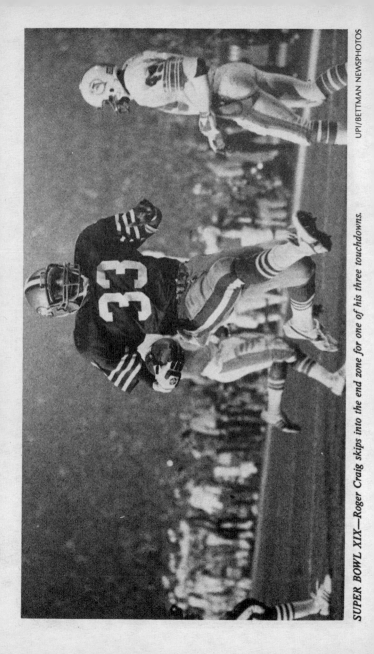

SUPER BOWL XIX—Roger Craig skips into the end zone for one of his three touchdowns.

SUPER BOWL XX—*Jim McMahon gets six points from the judges on his swan dive into the end zone.* UPI/BETTMAN NEWSPHOTOS

SUPER BOWL XXII—Ricky Sanders gathers in a Doug Williams pass, and it's off to the races.

SUPER BOWL XXIII—Jerry Rice flies high to snare a Montana pass.

MICHAEL ZAGARIS

SUPER BOWL XXIV—Joe Montana makes like Michael Jordan after firing third quarter touchdown pass.

SUPER BOWL XXV—O.J. Anderson getting the tough yardage.

SUPER BOWL XXVI—Mark Rypien ripping apart the Bills.

with less than seven minutes left, and some of the Steelers started celebrating on the sidelines.

But Dallas wasn't ready to give up. They went 89 yards in eight plays and scored on a 7-yard toss to Billy Joe DuPree with 2:23 left.

Gerela squibbed an onside kick, which the Steelers fumbled and Dallas pounced on. Staubach came out throwing and hit Drew Pearson for 22 yards and again for 25. Then he hit Butch Johnson for a 4-yard touchdown and the Steeler lead was down to 35-31.

There were 22 seconds left as both teams lined up for another onside kick. The ball skidded toward the Steeler line but this time Rocky Bleier fell on it. Pittsburgh had weathered the Cowboy cyclone and became the first team to win three Super Bowls.

After the game, and after all the seasons and all the victories, reporters were *still* asking if Terry Bradshaw had proven himself. Coach Noll looked at the reporters and said, "Terry had nothing to prove. He's quarterbacked three Super Bowl winners, and nobody else has done that."

Bradshaw, who was named the MVP while setting Super Bowl records for most yards passing (318), longest scoring pass (75 yards), and most touchdown passes, told reporters, "I don't think I had anything to prove. I learned this year that you don't play well unless you relax and let your abilities work for you. I decided that I wasn't going to let the pressure of the Super Bowl dictate to me. I was just going to play my game today."

And then he laughed. "This was an exciting game. This game was fun!"

SUPER BOWL XIV

January 20, 1980

PITTSBURGH
vs.
LOS ANGELES RAMS
"The Steel Curtain"

THE STEELERS HAD so much fun in Super Bowl XIII, they came back for the next one. They won their division with a 12-4 record and then mauled Miami, 34-14, and humbled Houston, 27-13, to capture the AFC title.

The Steeler offense had had a totally awesome season. They led the league in scoring with a team record of 416 points, while gaining 6,258 yards (an *average* of 391 per game!), just 31 yards short of the all-time record.

They struck by air and they struck on the ground. Bradshaw had a phenomenal year as he threw for 26 touchdowns and set Steeler records for completions (259) and yards (3,724). Stallworth set a Steeler record with 70 receptions and Swann, slowed by injuries, only caught 41, but his average of 19.7 yards per catch was the best of his career. And Franco Harris, with 1,186 rushing yards, recorded his seventh 1,000-yard season, tying the great Jim Brown's record. The line blocked like bulldozers, and Bennie Cunningham, the tight end, was healthy.

They had the Number-One defense in the AFC as Joe Greene and his friends up front formed the Steel Curtain that stopped the run and terrorized quarterbacks. Jack Lambert, the All-Pro middle line-backer, was all over the field making tackles and creating mayhem. In their play-off games, the Steeler defense had held Miami (with Csonka) and Houston (with Earl Campbell, the leading rusher in the NFL) to a *combined* total of only 49 yards rushing!

The Los Angeles Rams, 9-7, won the NFC West for the seventh straight year and then upset the Cowboys, 21-19. They went on to beat Tampa Bay, 9-0, in a game that *Sports Illustrated* called "a game for losers, played by losers" to earn a trip to the Super Bowl.

The Rams had struggled through a season of injuries and aggravation. But a second-string quarterback, Vince Ferragamo, had led them to six victories in their last seven games. Wide receiver Bill Waddy was a deep threat and a strong offensive line had helped Wendell Tyler run for 1,109 yards and fullback Cullen Bryant for 619.

Their defense—which had led the NFC in sacks with 52—was anchored at one end by Jack Young-blood, who had been an All-Pro for six seasons, and at the other end by hard-charging Fred Dryer. The line-backers were strong, especially "Hacksaw" Reynolds, and they had a very good secondary.

The Rams' seven losses were the most by any previous Super Bowl team and a lot of people didn't think that they belonged on the same field with the Steelers. One writer suggested that Terry Bradshaw should throw left-handed and that the Rams should be allowed to play with 12 men to make the game more competitive. The Ram players didn't find the criticism humorous. Doug France, their All-Pro offensive tackle, complained, "Everyone wrote us off in the play-offs. I thought we'd get more respect after those games, but we haven't. People act like we're not even supposed to be in the Super Bowl." Fred Dryer stared at a reporter and simply said, "The people who think the Steelers are going to walk all over us have another think coming."

The Steelers weren't taking them lightly. They had lost to the Rams in 1978, 1975, and 1971. In fact, they had beaten the Rams only once in the 12 times they had played each other. Dwight White noted that the Rams had overcome a lot of injuries and team problems. "They've made it to the Super Bowl, and people are still down on them. That will make them dangerous." "The Rams," noted Bradshaw, "are an outstanding team. They have a tremendous defense and they pose a lot of problems. We played them last year and they beat us, 10-7."

The Rams took the opening kickoff, but after running three plays, they were forced to punt. Pittsburgh moved on the ground for two first downs and then Bradshaw hit Harris over the middle with a 32-yard pass. But the Rams' defense dug in and Pittsburgh had to settle for a 41-yard field goal from rookie Matt Bahr.

A short kickoff gave the Rams terrific field position at their 41-yard line. Ferragamo passed to Tyler for 6 yards. On the next play, Tyler took a handoff and raced around left end, broke tackles, and headed for the end zone. Donnie Shell finally managed to drag him down at the 14, after a 39-yard gain (the longest run of the year against the startled Steelers). Five plays later, Cullen Bryant burst across the goal line and the Rams led, 7-3.

Larry Anderson gave Pittsburgh a big lift when he ran the kickoff back 45 yards to the Steeler 47. Bradshaw didn't want to let this opportunity slip away. He wanted to get in front of the Rams and not have to play catch-up against their defense. Terry handed off to Franco, who romped around right end for 12 yards. Bleier ran for 1, Cunningham caught an 8-yarder, and then Bleier struggled for 2 more—and another first down. Bradshaw next teamed up with Swann at the 18 as the first period ended.

In the second quarter, he hit Cunningham, again, at the 5. Harris hit the middle of the line for a 1-yard gain. Bradshaw then went for the score but the stubborn Rams stopped Stallworth at the 1. On third down, the Rams bunched up to stop a power play up the middle, but Bradshaw crossed them up by pitching out wide to Harris. Franco swept around the right side and scored standing up.

The Steelers led, 10-7, but Ferragamo led the Rams right back. Masterfully mixing passes with runs, and assisted by a pass-interference call against Donnie Shell, the Rams went 67 yards in ten plays that ended with a Frank Corral field goal to tie the game.

Anderson ran the ensuing kickoff back 38 yards to give the Steelers excellent field position once again, but they couldn't move the ball. After an exchange of punts, Bradshaw's pass was picked off by safety Dave Elmendorf and returned to the Steeler 39. Ferragamo passed the Rams into Pittsburgh territory but he was sacked by John Banaszak on a third-down play and they had to go for a field goal. Corral connected from the 45 and the Rams led the Steelers, 13-10, at the half.

In the locker room, assistant coach Woody Widenhofer yelled at the Steelers' defensive unit, "How can you mess up this way? You guys are standing out there like statues!"

The amazing Anderson took the second-half kickoff and gave the Steelers great field position for the third time by returning it 37 yards. Bradshaw lulled the Ram defense by keeping the ball on the ground for four plays. And then on second down, from the Rams' 47, he sent Swann long. Lynn leaped up at the 2-yard line, came down with the ball, and tumbled into the end zone as Pittsburgh retook the lead, 17-13.

But they didn't hold it. Ferragamo hit Bill Waddy with a 51-yard strike to the Steeler 24. On the next play, Vince handed off to Lawrence McCutcheon. McCutcheon started to sweep around the right side but as Pittsburgh came up to play the run, he stopped and delivered a strike to Ron Smith, who was all alone in the end zone. The extra point was missed but the team that just wouldn't quit had retaken the lead, 19-17.

The Steelers came out smoking but the Rams quickly put out their fire. First, Eddie Brown stopped a short drive with an interception. And then, after a punt, Bradshaw led Pittsburgh on a seven-play drive to the Rams' 16. But Rod Perry put an end to that threat when he picked off a pass intended for Stallworth.

After a booming punt had put Pittsburgh back on its own 25, Bradshaw faced a third and 8. If the Rams held, they could take control of the game. Terry called out the signals, took the snap, and set up to pass. Stallworth went straight up the field, faked to the outside, and then went deep down the middle. Bradshaw hung the ball up and Stallworth, going full speed, took it over his shoulder at the Ram 32, never breaking stride until he had completed an electrifying 73-yard play.

The Rams, trailing 24-19 with just under nine minutes remaining, rode three passes into Steeler territory. Ferragamo then saw Smith open in the end zone but Jack Lambert dropped back and made a critical interception that preserved the Steeler lead.

Faced with a third and 7 late in the fourth period, Bradshaw found the Rams in a short-pass defense. So he sent Stallworth on a deep pattern, and his talented teammate again made an incredible over-the-head catch, before slipping down at the LA 22. A pass-interference call gave Pittsburgh the ball at the 1-yard line. Bleier got the call but the Ram defense threw him back. Harris hit the line but couldn't budge it. On third down with less than two minutes left in the game, Harris finally punched across the score that gave Pittsburgh the game, 31-19.

The Rams were disappointed but proud of their effort. Fred Dryer expressed their feelings when he said, "I guarantee those guys know they've been in a football game."

The Steelers had won their fourth Super Bowl and were being ranked with the greatest teams of all time. Asked if this were the best team of all time, coach Chuck Noll replied, "I don't have to say it. The Steelers have proven themselves."

SUPER BOWL XV

January 25, 1981

OAKLAND
VS.
PHILADELPHIA

"Their Finest Hour"

THE PHILADELPHIA EAGLES won the NFC East with a record of 13-3, and then mangled Minnesota, 31-16, and dumped Dallas, 20-7, to earn a trip to New Orleans and their first appearance in a Super Bowl.

The offense featured quarterback Ron Jaworski, who was the leading passer in the NFL. Wilbert Montgomery was one of the top halfbacks in the league. After two successive years in which he gained more than 1,200 yards, injuries had limited Montgomery to only 778 yards. But he showed that he was fully recovered by rushing for 194 yards against the Cowboys in the NFC championship game. Wilbert was also a fine receiver coming out of the backfield, but their deep threat was 6'7" Harold Carmichael.

They had a tough defense that had only given up 222 points, the lowest figure in the NFL. Charlie Johnson anchored the line at nose tackle. Their linebackers, led by Bill Bergey and Jerry Robinson, were quick and loved to hit. The secondary was very solid, especially at the corners, which were manned by Herman Edwards and rookie Roynell Young. The Eagles had played and beaten Oakland, 10-7, during the season, and the defense had sacked Jim Plunkett eight times!

The Oakland Raiders finished second in the AFC West and made the play-offs as a wild-card team with an 11-5 record. They reached the Super Bowl by pulling off three straight upsets in the play-offs: 27-7 over Houston, 14-12 over Cleveland, and 34-27 over San Diego.

After being in the play-offs for six consecutive years, the Raiders had missed out in 1978 and 1979. In 1980, they were picked to finish last and they seemed to be fulfilling the prediction as their record fell to 2-3, and their quarterback, Dan Pastorini, went down for the season with a broken leg.

After that game, Art Shell, their All-Pro tackle, called a "players-only" meeting. "We know," he told them, "that we have better talent than our performances indicate." And then he reminded the other players about what John Madden used to say when he was the coach. "If you're not going to help us, then move aside because we're coming through."

They would have to get through, though, with Jim Plunkett, a veteran reserve quarterback who had not thrown a single pass in 1978 and only 15 in 1979.

Plunkett came through splendidly by supplying the passing and the leadership that the team needed to win 9 of its last 11 games and 3 more in the playoffs! Wide receivers Cliff Branch and Bob Chandler and tight end Raymond Chester caught most of the passes, while Mark Van Eegen and Kenny King did most of the running.

The Raider defense, as usual, was punishing. They were especially strong on the left side with cornerback Lester Hayes, who led the league with 13 interceptions; Ted "The Mad Stork" Hendricks at linebacker; and giant (6'8", 280 pounds) John Matuszak at end. Hendricks was a one-man team. As one opposing coach said, "It's hard to figure out what to do against him. He plays the run, covers a back on a pass pattern, and can blitz the quarterback!" As for Matuszak, he was so strong, said one player, "I've seen him take on a triple-team and just bust it wide open."

The Raiders jumped out to a quick 7-0 lead when Plunkett hit Branch with a two-yard pass after a short drive that began after linebacker Ron Martin intercepted Jaworski's first pass of the game.

Neither team mounted much of an offense for most of the first quarter, but as it drew to a close, the Raiders struck suddenly. Plunkett hit Branch for a short gain; King ran for 2 to the Oakland 20; Plunkett, scrambling away from a pass rush, hit King at the 39. King slipped a tackle by Herman Edwards and raced 61 yards down the sideline for a record-setting 80-yard touchdown. "It was supposed to be a 6-yard play," said King. "But when Jim scrambled, the linebacker dropped me and went for Jim and he got me the ball. He made an amazing throw."

Jaworski led the Eagles on a drive early in the second quarter that stalled at the 13, so Tony Franklin kicked a 30-yard field goal to cut the lead to 14-3. The defense dominated again, until late in the quarter, when Jaworski led the Eagles on a 62-yard drive to the Oakland 11. With 54 seconds left, Franklin tried a 28-yard field goal, but Hendricks crashed in, stuck up one of his long arms, and blocked the ball.

The Raiders took the second half kickoff and again, like a coiled snake, struck quickly. Plunkett hit King for 13 and Chandler for 32. And after a 4-yard run by Van Eeghen moved the ball to the Philadelphia 29, Plunkett rifled a pass to Cliff Branch, who wrestled it away from Roynell Young in the end zone to give the Raiders a 21-3 lead.

The Raiders had put Philadelphia in a deep hole and they made it even deeper when Ron Martin intercepted Jaworski for the second time. Bahr made the Eagles pay for the mistake when he kicked a field goal after Plunkett moved the Raiders into position by passing twice to Raymond Chester, once for 16 yards and then again for 17.

The Eagles finally managed to score a touchdown in the fourth quarter when Jaworski hit tight end Keith Krepfle with an 8-yarder to cut the lead to 24-10. But the Raiders didn't let them get on a roll. They marched from their 11 to the Eagle 17 and when the drive stalled, Bahr kicked his third field goal to stretch the lead to 27-10.

On their following possession, Jaworski lost a fumble and on their next and last one, Martin set a new Super Bowl record by recording his third interception. The renegade Raiders had clipped the Eagles' wings.

Philadelphia had never actually gotten into the game. "We never got our motor running," said John Spagnola. "The whole game just seemed to have come and gone. It just seems like a nightmare."

To the Raiders, and especially to MVP Jim Plunkett, it seemed like a dream come true. "This," he said, "is my great moment as a professional. I'm just so proud to be a member of this team."

Gene Upshaw, the only Raider to have played on all three Super Bowl teams, recalled the struggle. "It was us against the world, and everybody said we didn't have a chance. If we played next week, we'd be picked to lose."

As Al Davis accepted the Vince Lombardi Trophy from Pete Rozelle, he looked around the locker room and announced, "This is the finest hour in the history of the Oakland Raiders."

SUPER BOWL XVI

January 24, 1982

SAN FRANCISCO
vs.
CINCINNATI

"Showdown at the Silverdome"

THE SAN FRANCISCO 49ers had the best record in the NFL at 13-3. They beat the Giants, 38-24, in the first play-off game and then defeated Dallas, 28-27, on a last-minute pass to win the NFC championship.

The 49ers' rise to the top caught everybody by surprise since their record the season before was only 6-10.

San Francisco had improved a lot on offense because of the development of their third-year quarterback, Joe Montana. Montana had had a sensational season and it was his last-minute pass to Dwight Clark that had earned the 49ers their one-point victory over Dallas. His coach, Bill Walsh, who had helped develop other top quarterbacks such as Kenny Anderson and Dan Fouts, said of Montana, ".'He may have the greatest football instincts I have ever seen. He's already the best at rolling out, avoiding the rush, and still finding his primary receiver." And Joe needed all of those instincts to direct the wide-open attack that Walsh designed.

Montana's favorite targets were his wide receivers, Dwight Clark (85 receptions) and Freddie Solomon (59); and running back Earl Cooper (51). The 49ers' top running backs were Cooper and Ricky Patton. They ran behind a strong offensive line led by center Fred Quillan and guard Randy Cross.

The 49ers had also made great improvement in their defense, and the most noticeable change was in the secondary where they started three rookies; Ronnie Lott, Eric Wright, and Carlton Williamson, who joined third-year man Dwight Hicks. Lott had made seven interceptions and run three of them back for touchdowns to tie an NFL record. He was also a ferocious hitter who had forced four fumbles. The defense also benefited greatly from Walsh's acquisition of two veterans, middle linebacker Jack "Hacksaw" Reynolds, and end Fred Dean, who specialized in sacking quarterbacks.

The Cincinnati Bengals had the best record, 12-4, in the AFC and advanced to the Super Bowl by beating Buffalo, 28-21, and spanking San Diego, 27-7. Cincinnati's development was also a surprise given the fact that they too had finished with a 6-10 record the previous season.

Kenny Anderson, an 11-year veteran, was the top-rated quarterback in the league. In answering a reporter's question about Anderson's abilities, Bill Walsh said, "He's big, he's strong. He runs extremely well and he's a great passer."

He also had great targets, such as tight end Dan Ross (71 receptions), rookie wide receiver Cris Collinsworth (67 receptions for 1,009 yards and eight touchdowns), and running back Pete Johnson (46 receptions). At 250 pounds, Johnson was a punishing inside runner who had gained more than 1,000 yards on the ground. Many experts thought that Johnson's running could provide the difference between these two evenly matched teams. The offensive line was anchored by left tackle Anthony Munoz, who had been selected as NFL offensive lineman of the year.

Cincinnati also had a fine defensive unit, which hadn't yielded more than 30 points in any of their 18 games, including play-offs. The pressure on the line came from ends Ross Browner and Eddie Edwards. And they had a solid secondary led by corner backs Louis Breeden and Ken Riley.

The 49ers won the toss but they fumbled the kickoff. The Bengals recovered on the 26-yard line and quickly moved to the 5 as Anderson connected with wide receiver Isaac Curtis for 8 and Ross for 11, sandwiched around a 2-yard run by Johnson. Anderson tried to come back to Curtis for the touchdown, but Dwight Hicks made a clutch interception and ran the ball out to the 32-yard line.

Montana moved the 49ers into Bengal territory by completing his first three passes. Then the 49ers brought the crowd at Pontiac Stadium to its feet when they ran a double-reverse flea-flicker that ended with Montana's hitting tight end Charles Young for a 14-yard gain to the Cincinnati 33. Three runs and a 14-yard pass to Solomon moved the ball to the 1-yard line and Montana took it in from there to give San Francisco a 7-0 lead.

The Bengals threatened later in the period when Collinsworth caught a 19-yard pass at the San Francisco eight-yard line. But Eric Wright tackled Collinsworth, stripped the ball out of his hands, and the 49ers recovered the fumble.

In the second period, the 49ers struck pay dirt again the first time they had the ball. Montana led them on a 92-yard touchdown drive—a new Super Bowl record —that ended with an 11-yard play-action pass to Earl Cooper, who circled out of the backfield. Montana had kept the drive alive with two key third-down passes: a 20-yarder to Solomon when the 49ers were way back on their own 11, and a 12-yard strike to Clark at the Cincinnati 31.

With just over four minutes left in the half, the 49ers went looking for more points. Montana hit Clark for 17 yards out to the Bengal 49, and Ricky Patton ran twice to advance the ball to the 39. Montana went back to Clark for another first down and then Solomon grabbed one at the 5. Montana missed his next two passes but Ray Wersching came in and kicked a 22-yard field goal that increased the 49ers' lead to 17-0.

Wersching kicked off with 15 seconds left in the half but lightning struck again—only this time, it was Cincinnati that fumbled. The 49ers recovered and Wersching kicked his second field goal to extend their lead to 20-0. The Bengals looked beat!

During the intermission, Walsh told the 49ers, "I'm not comfortable with this lead. We're playing a great team. Don't coast. Go out there and play like it's 0-0, or Anderson will burn us."

Bengal coach Forest Gregg reminded his team that they had been behind before and come back to win.

"We came from 21-down to beat Seattle. Just go out and play better."

The Bengals took their coach's advice on the second-half kickoff, and marched 83 yards in nine plays. Anderson scored the touchdown on a 5-yard run to narrow the gap to 20-7. In the middle of the period, Anderson did burn San Francisco, as Walsh had warned, when he hit Collinsworth with a 49-yard strike down to the 14. Pete Johnson crashed to the 3 on a daring fourth-down play to give the Bengals a first-and-goal. Then Johnson bucked straight ahead for 2 yards. But on second down, John Harty met him head-on and stopped him for no gain. On third down, Anderson tried to cross up the 49ers by swinging a pass out to Charles Alexander in the right flat. But linebacker Dan Bunz read the play and dropped Alexander at the 1. On fourth down, the Bengals decided to go for the touchdown. Johnson took the hand-off and tried to bust through for the score but he was met by Reynolds and Lott and knocked back. The 49ers had made a great goal-line stand!

The Bengals came back early in the fourth quarter, though, as Anderson tossed a four-yard pass to Ross to cut the score to 20-14. They were only a touchdown and an extra point away from the lead.

The 49ers wanted to increase their lead and to keep the ball on the ground to use up the clock. They did both as they ran seven times in a ten-play drive that positioned Wersching for his third field goal, a 40-yarder, that made the score 23-14.

The Bengals needed two scores now and with only five minutes left, Anderson had to pass. The 49ers were ready, though, and Eric Wright swooped in and came up with an interception. A few plays later, Wersching kicked his fourth field goal and the 49ers led, 26-14.

There were less than two minutes left but the Bengals didn't quit. Anderson hit on six consecutive passes, the last one a three-yard touchdown to Dan Ross. Then the Bengals tried an onside kick but Dwight White caught the ball. Joe Montana, who was selected as the game's MVP, took one last snap, time ran out, the game was history.

Before the Super Bowl, Bill Walsh, the 49ers' coach, had told reporters, "The Super Bowl overemphasizes winning and losing. The losing team shouldn't feel like it has to hide its head."

After the game, in a traditional gesture, the President of the United States called to congratulate the coach of the winning team.

After he had taken the call, Walsh was asked if the President should also call the losing team. "Darn right," replied Walsh. "It's a good idea."

SUPER BOWL XVII

January 30, 1983

WASHINGTON vs. MIAMI
"Hog-Tied"

IN A SEASON shortened by a labor dispute between the players and the owners, the Washington Redskins compiled an 8-1 record, the best record in the NFC.

Because of the shortened season, the play-off system was expanded to three rounds. In the first round, the 'Skins defeated Detroit, 31-7. In the second round, they mashed Minnesota, 21-7; and in the NFC championship game, they downed Dallas, 31-17.

Joe Theismann had finished the season as the top-rated quarterback in the NFC. He had a good arm and he also scrambled well. His top receivers were Charlie Brown and Alvin Garrett, who was playing in the place of the great Art Monk, sidelined with an injury. Brown, 5'11", and Garrett, at 5'7", were known as the Smurfs because of their size. But they certainly didn't play small. Brown had caught 43 passes (8 for touchdowns) in Washington's 12 games, and Garrett, who caught only 1 pass during the season, added 13 (4 for touchdowns) during the play-offs!

But Washington's main man on offense was fullback John Riggins. Including the play-offs, John had rushed for 997 yards and six touchdowns and, as Theismann pointed out, "When he runs, it opens up our game. It makes our passing game more effective." Before the first play-off game, John had gone to coach Joe Gibbs and said, "If we're going to get to the Super Bowl, then I need the ball more." Gibbs gave him the ball and big John rushed 98 times in the three play-off games and produced 444 yards! The offensive line that did the blocking was called, affectionately, "The Hogs."

The defense was very strong. Dave Butz, a mountain of a man at 6'7" and 295 pounds, clogged up the middle and made it difficult to run against Washington. When the opposition wanted to pass, they often found Dexter Manley and Tony McGee, who each had 6 1/2 sacks, in their face.

The Miami Dolphins, with a 7-2 record, finished second in the AFC to the Raiders. (Because of the short season, there wasn't any divisional play. The top eight teams in each conference qualified for the play-offs.) Miami beat New England, 28-13, socked San Diego, 34-13, and then shut out the New York Jets, 14-0.

David Woodley was an average quarterback, and his main receivers were also average. The offensive line, though, was exceptionally strong. It protected Woodley well and opened up the holes for fullback Andra Franklin, who finished second in the AFC with 701 yards. He added 252 in the play-offs and scored nine touchdowns in Miami's 12 games. Tony Nathan was a good, all-purpose back who could run and catch passes effectively. The plan was to establish the run and then go deep with the pass.

Their main strength was the defense, which was rated the best in the league. They were known as "The Killer Bees" because they were fast and their "sting" was "deadly." Also, 6 of the 11 starters had last names that began with the letter *B*.

Bob Baumhower, an All-Pro, was an outstanding nose tackle, who made running against Miami a difficult task. A. J. Duhe, who combined great strength with good speed, lined up all over the field to confuse offenses and to be at the point of attack. The secondary was very strong. Corner backs Don McNeal and Gerald Small and the safeties, brothers Lyle and Glen Blackwood, covered receivers like a blanket and were also excellent at stopping the run.

Miami was favored, but John Madden picked Washington, a team that had 26 free agents—players that no other team wanted—on their 45-man roster. Fourteen of them had never even been drafted by an NFL team! "What winning a game like this is all about is controlling the line of scrimmage, and Washington will do that," said Madden. "Which means that John Riggins will run effectively and that will make Theismann more effective."

Miami received the kickoff but after running three plays, they were forced to punt. Washington picked up a first down on three runs by Riggins and another on a pass to Brown. But then they were also forced to punt.

Miami took over on its own 20, and Tony Nathan ran for 4. On second down, wide receiver Jimmy Cefalo went in motion to his right. Woodley took the snap, faked a pitch-out, looked downfield to his left, and then turned and delivered a perfect pass to a wide-open Cefalo. With nothing but open field in front of him, Jimmy raced the last 31 yards into the end zone to complete a 76-yard touchdown play! Miami had gone deep and led the deflated Redskins, 7-0.

Later in the period, Miami was moving well with the run when Woodley decided to go deep again. But before he could release the ball, he was decked by Dexter Manley, which caused Woodley to fumble. Dave Butz recovered the ball and, a few plays later, Mark Mosely kicked a field goal that cut Miami's lead to 7-3.

Fulton Walker took the kickoff on his 5-yard line and ran it all the way back to Miami's 47. The Dolphins stayed mostly on the ground as they moved to a first down at the Washington 8-yard line. The Redskins' defense tightened up, though, and the Dolphins had to settle for a Uwe Von Schamann field goal and a 10-3 lead.

With just under six minutes left in the half, the Redskins began to roll when Rick Walker hauled in a 27-yard pass from Theismann. Joe mixed passes with runs and added a 12-yard scramble of his own to lead the Redskins down to the 4. Then he found Alvin Garrett, the smallest Smurf, free in the end zone, and lobbed a perfect pass over Gerald Small's head. The score was tied, 10-10, with less than two minutes left in the half.

The marching bands got set to take the field, but Fulton Walker gave the crowd at the Rose Bowl a different type of entertainment when he gathered in the kickoff and raced through the Redskins' coverage for a 98-yard touchdown! Walker's explosive run marked the first time in Super Bowl history that a kickoff had been returned for a touchdown, and it gave Miami the lead again at 17-10.

During the intermission, Gibbs told the Redskins

that they had played well and would turn the game around. "I had a good feeling."

Early in the second half, Washington moved to a first down on their own 47, and then it was their turn to bring the crowd to its feet. They surprised Miami with a reverse and Garrett raced—or smurfed—44 yards before he was tackled at the 9. They only managed to move the ball to the 6, however, and had to settle for another Mosley field goal that cut the Dolphins' lead to 17-13.

Later in the period, after Theismann had been intercepted, Miami moved the ball to the Washington 37. Woodley went deep for Cefalo again, but Redskins' cornerback Vernon Dean tipped the ball and safety Mark Murphy made a one-handed interception as he fell to the ground. The Redskins rode Theismann's throws and Riggins' runs into Dolphin territory. Then they pulled another trick play, a flea-flicker from Theismann to Riggins and back to Theismann. The only problem was that Miami wasn't fooled and Lyle Blackwood made a diving interception at the 1-yard line.

Washington played tough defense, though, and Miami had to punt from deep in their own territory. The Redskins ran Riggins twice and Clarence Harmon once but came up a yard short at the Dolphin 43. Coach Gibbs decided to take the gamble and go for the first down. The Dolphins lined up in a ten-man front with only Don McNeal playing back. The Redskins sent a receiver in motion to confuse McNeal, and Theismann handed the ball off to Riggins. Big John moved to his left while looking for day-light and then cut to the outside. McNeal made a grab at him but John pushed him off with a straight arm, and raced 43 yards into the end zone to give Washington their first lead of the game, 20-17.

The Redskins' defense soon forced another punt and Mike Nelms's 12-yard return gave them excellent field position at the Miami 41. Riggins moved the ball to the 23 with five straight runs. After three more runs, Theismann rolled left and hit Brown at the 9 with a big third-down pass. Riggins moved the ball to the six-yard line on two carries as the two-minute warning was given. On third down, Theismann rolled out to his right and searched the end zone for an open receiver. He saw Brown break free and hit him with a pass just before Charlie crossed the sideline stripe. The Redskins had the score and the game, 27-17.

The Redskins' defense had totally dominated Miami in the second half, allowing only two first downs and no completions!

John Riggins, who was named the MVP, set new Super Bowl records for carries (38), yards gained rushing (166), and longest scoring run from scrimmage (43 yards). He told reporters "I'm very happy, but I'm very tired. I told Joe Gibbs I wanted the ball, but I think he got a little carried away."

SUPER BOWL XVIII

January 22, 1984

LOS ANGELES RAIDERS
vs.
WASHINGTON REDSKINS

"Domination!"

THE REDSKINS ROARED through the regular season
with a 14-2 record, the best in the entire NFL. In
the play-offs they routed the Rams, 51-7, and then
just barely squeezed by the 49ers, 24-21, when Mark
Mosley kicked a field goal with 40 seconds left in the
game.

The Redskins appeared to be even better than last
year. They were the first NFC team ever to win 14
games during the regular season and their two losses
were by only one point each. They had been played
tough by the 49ers but they had held on and were
riding an 11-game winning streak into the Super Bowl
at Tampa Stadium.

Their offense set a league record by scoring 541
points. Riggins ran for well over 1,000 yards, set a

record by scoring 24 touchdowns, and then added 5 more in the two play-off games! Theismann was selected as the MVP and Charlie Brown tied for the conference lead with 78 receptions. Art Monk was healthy and so was Joe Washington, their second-leading ground gainer and third-leading pass receiver. And helping to make all this possible was the fine offensive line known as "The Hogs."

The defense had been the best in the NFL against the rush, but they did have some problems with the passing game. But who's perfect?

The Los Angeles Raiders (they had moved from Oakland in 1982) won the AFC West with a 12-4 record. Then they pounded Pittsburgh, 38-10, and squashed Seattle, a team that had beaten them twice during the season, 30-14, to win the AFC title.

Jim Plunkett, who had just finished his finest season, had great receivers: tight end Todd Christensen had led the league with 92 receptions and Cliff Branch and Malcolm Barnwell both had the speed to go deep. The real jewel, however, was halfback Marcus Allen. He had rushed for 1,014 yards (plus 275 more in the playoffs), caught 68 passes, and scored 12 touchdowns. The line was very strong at pass-blocking and run-blocking.

The Raiders also had a ferocious defense. Their three-man front was led by Pro-Bowlers Howie Long and Lyle Alzado. They had a fine group of linebackers, led by another Pro-Bowl pick, Ron Martin, and Matt Millen. And they had the two best cornerbacks in the league, Lester Hayes and Mark Haynes. In the AFC title game, they had held Curt Warner, the conference rushing leader, to 26 yards in 11 carries.

Coach Tom Flores explained the way the Raiders

played. "We attack—on offense, on defense, on special teams."

Most people expected this to be a very tough, close game, like the thrilling game that the teams had played in the fifth week of the season when the Redskins won, 37-35, by scoring 17 points in the last six minutes of the game.

After the Raiders gained a first down on the first series of the game, they were forced to punt. The Redskins also managed a first down before they had to bring on the punting team. As the teams lined up, the Raiders shifted Lester Hayes from the left side (his usual position), to the right side, which confused Washington's punting unit. That little bit of uncertainty was all that Derrick Jensen needed to break through and block the punt. Then he chased the ball into the end zone and fell on it to give LA a 7-0 lead. It was the only blocked punt that Washington had given up in the last three years!

In the second quarter, the Raiders struck quickly. Branch went deep and beat double coverage to haul in a 50-yard pass from Plunkett. After LA picked up three yards on a running play, Plunkett faked another handoff while Branch faked corner back Anthony Washington to the outside, and then cut over the middle. Plunkett hit Branch on his break and the Raiders led, 14-0. As Branch explained the play, "We saw the 49ers beat Anthony with corner patterns and we knew that he would be thinking about it. So we gave him the same look—we knew he'd bite—and then went inside."

Washington then marched 73 yards, with Theismann hitting Clint Didier for 18 and 20 yards and Alvin Garrett for 17. But they were stopped at the 7, and had to settle for a Mark Moseley field goal.

Washington had the ball with only 12 seconds left in the half and coach Joe Gibbs decided to try a screen pass to Joe Washington, the same play that had worked for 67 yards against the Raiders in their game during the season. But a Raider coach also remembered the play so he sent in Jack Squirek, a 6'4" linebacker and told him to forget everyone else and just stay with Joe Washington. Theismann lobbed the ball over Alzado's head toward Washington, but Squirek knifed in for the interception and a 5-yard touchdown run. "It felt like a dream," Squirek said. "I couldn't believe it until everybody started pounding me in the end zone."

Despite the fact that they were down by 21-3, the Redskins were confident that they could come back against LA the way they had in the earlier game.

Garrett ran the second-half kickoff back 35 yards and then Theismann hit Charlie Brown for 23. The Redskins were rolling and they didn't stop until Riggins had completed the 70-yard drive with a 1-yard touchdown run. The extra point failed, but they had cut the score to 21-9.

This was a key series. If the Washington defense could shut LA down, the momentum would shift toward Washington. But the Redskins couldn't contain the outside speed of the Raiders. Cornell Green was hit with a 38-yard pass-interference penalty while trying to stay with Barnwell, and six plays later, Marcus Allen carried it in from the 5 to up the score to 28-9.

Washington had one last opportunity late in the third quarter when they recovered a Cliff Branch fumble on the LA 35-yard line. They moved 9 yards and faced a fourth-and-1, as they had against Miami last year. Once again, they gave the ball to Riggins and once again he slid along the line to his left, looking for daylight. But this time, all he found was the black jersey of Rod Martin who cut him down for no gain.

The Raiders took over on their own 26 and, on the last play of the third quarter, Plunkett handed off to Marcus Allen. Allen started to his left, saw a lot of red jerseys, cut back up the middle, and—whoosh—was gone: 74 yards for the longest run from scrimmage in Super Bowl history.

In the final quarter, the Raiders sacked Theismann three times, made him fumble once, and intercepted a pass. Allen ripped off a 39-yard run to help set up a Chris Bahr field goal, as the Raiders routed the Redskins, 38-9. The Raiders' 38 points were the most ever scored by one team in the Super Bowl, and the margin of victory was also the largest.

Allen, who set a new Super Bowl record by rushing for 191 yards, was named the Most Valuable Player. The defensive effort—keyed by the play of Hayes and Haynes—had played a vital role in the victory. They were so good that they shut down the passing game and let the linebackers concentrate on helping the line stop Riggins.

The Raider locker room was a happy scene as Al Davis accepted the Vince Lombardi Trophy from NFL commissioner Pete Rozelle. Davis declared that this was the "greatest Raider team of all time." And who could argue? They had just played a really fine team and as coach Tom Flores put it, "We dominated them."

SUPER BOWL XIX

January 20, 1985

SAN FRANCISCO vs. MIAMI
"Montana Magic"

MIAMI WON THE AFC with the second-best record, 14-2, in the entire NFL. Then they socked Seattle, 31-10, and pulverized Pittsburgh, 45-28, to earn a trip to Stanford Stadium and the franchise's fifth appearance in the Super Bowl.

The Dolphins led the league in scoring with 513 points and the main reason was Dan Marino. Marino, in only his second year in the NFL, had the most sensational season that any quarterback had ever had. He virtually rewrote the record book as he set five NFL passing records. He became the first quarterback to throw for more than 5,000 yards by gaining 5,084 and he threw for 48 touchdowns (the old record, which he left in the dust, was 36). He also set records for completions (362), number of games passing for

300 yards or more (nine), and most games passing for 400 yards or more (four).

Marino was so good because of how quickly he set up, read the defense, and threw. He had the fastest release that anyone had ever seen, which made it hard for opponents to sack him. Another reason—he was sacked only 13 times during the season and not at all in the play-offs when defenses are usually tougher—was because he played behind a great line, led by All-Pro center Dwight Stephenson. As the 49ers' defensive coach said, "They have the hardest-working offensive line I've ever seen."

Given time, Marino usually found his receivers, and in Mark Clayton and Mark "Super" Duper (together they were known as the "Marks Brothers"), he had one of the best sets of receivers ever. Clayton had 73 catches, including an NFL record 18 touchdowns, while Duper had 71 receptions, 8 for touchdowns. Each of them gained more than 1,300 yards in receptions, marking the first time that any team had two receivers who each gained more than 1,300 yards in the same season. The leading rushers for Miami were fullback Woody Bennett (606 yards) and Tony Nathan (558 yards and 61 receptions).

The San Francisco 49ers had the best record in the NFL (15-1) and became the first team ever to win 15 games in the regular season. Then they cut down the Giants, 21-10, and blanked the Chicago Bears, 23-0, to make it to the Super Bowl.

The 49ers' offense, which led the NFC with 475 points, had great balance between its passing and running games. The offense was directed on the field by a great quarterback, Joe Montana. Joe had led the NFC in passing while throwing for 3,630 yards, 28 touchdowns, and only ten interceptions. Montana created a lot of excitement by scrambling and throwing on the run, and always seemed to make the big play when it was needed.

Montana had plenty of help from halfback Wendell Tyler, who rushed for a team record of 1,262 yards, and fullback Roger Craig, who rushed for 649 yards and added another 675 yards on 71 receptions (tops on the 49ers) while scoring ten touchdowns. The other main receivers were Freddie Solomon, their deep threat, who caught 40 passes, ten for touchdowns; Dwight Clark, 52 catches, six for touchdowns; and tight end Earl Cooper, 41 catches and four touchdowns.

They had a fine offensive line that included tackles Keith Fanhorst, John Ayres, Bubba Paris, Randy Cross, and Fred Quillan.

The 49ers also had a tremendous defense that had allowed the fewest points (227) in the league. They rotated their linemen, depending upon whether they thought their opponents would run or pass. Their linebacking, led by All-Pro Keena Turner, was strong, and their defensive backs were exceptional. All four of them—corner backs Ronnie Lott and Eric Wright, and safeties Carlton Williamson and Dwight Hicks—had been selected to play in the Pro Bowl!

Marino had had a great season and two great play-off games—683 yards and seven touchdown passes—and had passed for at least one touchdown in 22 consecutive games!

Montana had had a terrific season, but not anywhere near as sensational as Marino's, and he had thrown five interceptions in the two play-off games. Dan was hot and Joe was not.

As a result, the Dolphins, especially Marino, got most of the publicity and attention from reporters and broadcasters. After a while, that got to bother even Montana—a basically shy and modest person who doesn't ask for a lot of attention—and the rest of the 49ers. Said Joe, "You don't mind being overlooked that much, but sometimes the reporters forgot there were two teams in the game. It got to all of us."

The 49ers' offensive game plan called for them to run a lot to their left side where they felt that 295-pound tackle Bubba Paris would be too much for Kim Bokamper. They also planned to use their backs as receivers against the inexperienced Miami linebackers. Their defensive plan was to double-team center Dwight Stephenson, which they felt would allow them to break through and pressure Marino.

After the 49ers were forced to punt, Miami took over, and as Marino hunched over his center, barking out the signals, a surge of excitement flashed through the fans at Stanford Stadium.

And Dan didn't disappoint them as he fired a 25-yard completion to Tony Nathan on their very first play. Five plays later, a pass to Clayton left Miami 2 yards short of the first down but Uwe Von Schamann kicked a 37-yard field goal to give them a 3-0 lead.

The 49ers came right back, though, with an eight-play, 78-yard drive, as Montana kept the Dolphin defense off balance with a diversified attack. First he passed short to Roger Craig, then two plays later, Tyler ran for a first down. On a third-down play, Montana rolled to his right, looking to pass. But he couldn't find an open receiver, so he cut back to his left and scrambled 15 yards for another first down at Miami's 33. On the next play, Montana again rolled right and spotted reserve running back Carl Monroe at the 15. He threw a beautiful pass over a defender's head and Monroe made the catch and beat two other Dolphin defenders to the end zone to give the 49ers a 7-3 lead.

But the Dolphins struck back quickly as Marino hit five consecutive passes, including two to Clayton (for 18 and 13 yards) and one to Duper (for 11) and two to tight end Dan Johnson, first for 21 yards and then a 2-yarder for the score as Miami retook the lead, 10-7. Coach Shula had directed Marino to call the plays at the line of scrimmage without a huddle so that the 49ers couldn't send in their various defensive specialists like pass rushers Fred Dean and Gary "Big Hands" Johnson.

After the touchdown, the 49ers countered that strategy with some of their own. They left Dean and Johnson in on almost every play and changed to a four-man rush to put even more pressure on Marino. And they took out one of their three linebackers and added a fifth defensive back to help cover the receivers.

The strategy began to work and neither team scored again until early in the second period. The 49ers had the ball on the Miami 47 and then just like that, Montana scrambled for 19 and then threw a 16-yard strike to Clark at the 12. Then, after a 4-yard run, Montana hit Craig at the 3 and Roger took it in to give the 49ers a 14-10 lead.

Miami had to punt again as Marino threw two incompletions, and Dana McLemore gave the 49ers excellent field position with a 29-yard return to San Francisco's 45-yard line. Tyler ran right for 9, and Craig ran left for 6. Montana threw to tight end Russ Francis for 10 yards and then again for 19 and a first down at the 11. Craig ran for 5 and then Montana went back to pass, dodged a blitz, and scrambled for the touchdown and a 21-10 lead.

After one running play and two incompletions,

Miami had to punt again and McLemore returned it to the 49ers' 48. Montana kept the Miami defense off guard as he mixed runs with passes and Craig capped the nine-play drive with a two-yard run behind a bruising block from Tyler. Craig had his second touchdown and the 49ers led, 28-10.

With only two minutes left in the half, Marino was given good protection and connected on seven passes, including a 30-yarder to tight end Joe Rose, to move the ball down to the 12. But after two incomplete passes and one for no gain, Miami had to settle for a field goal. With only 12 seconds left in the half, the Dolphins received a break when the 49ers fumbled the kickoff and von Schamann added another 3-pointer to cut the lead to 28-16 at half time.

Any thoughts of a Miami comeback in the second half were quickly put to rest, though, as the 49ers sacked Marino on third down, and then they took the punt, marched 43 yards, and scored on a Ray Wersching field goal.

On the Dolphins' next possession, Marino was sacked two more times and Miami was forced to punt again. On first down from his 30, Montana hit Tyler over the middle for 40 yards and then hit Francis for 14. Three plays later, Craig had his third touchdown on a 16-yard pass from Montana, as the 49ers upped their lead to 38-16 and closed out the scoring. The defense, though, wasn't finished. The next time Miami had the ball, Eric Wright intercepted Marino and two possessions later, Carlton Williamson also picked one off.

After the game, Marino, who had been intercepted twice and sacked four times—the most in his career— was glum. "We knew what we had to do but they took us right out of our game." Defensive end Doug Betters was shocked at the outcome. "The 49ers drilled us. Nobody ever did to us what they did to us." And Coach Shula put it simply, "We were dominated."

The 49ers set a bunch of Super Bowl records, including most yards gained (537); Montana, who was selected as MVP, set Super Bowl records for passing yardage (331) and rushing yardage by a quarterback (59).

But it was the defense that pressured Marino and shut off his receivers to turn the game around. As many football experts will tell you, offense may excite the crowds, but most championship games are won by the defense.

Before the game, Joe Namath had been asked his opinion about the quarterbacks. "Marino is the best passer I've ever seen, but if I want to win one game, I'll go with Montana."

SUPER BOWL XX

January 26, 1986

CHICAGO vs. NEW ENGLAND
"Dented"

THE CHICAGO BEARS romped to the NFC Central Division title with a 15-1 record, the best in the NFL. Then they toppled the Giants, 21-0, and routed the Rams, 24-0, to win a trip to New Orleans.

The Bears were bursting with talent. Mike Ditka had been named Coach of the Year, linebacker Mike Singletary had been selected as Defensive Player of the Year, and halfback Walter Payton had been selected as Offensive Player of the Year. The offense led the league in rushing and scored 456 points, and the defense gave up the fewest points (198) and allowed the fewest yards (258.4 per game).

Payton, the all-time leading rusher in the NFL (14,860 yards), had rushed for 1,551 yards during the season and also led the team in receptions with 52.

Payton combined great speed with great power. Referring to the speed, New England linebacker Steve Nelson said, "You think you've got him and then he goes into a second gear." And some of the people who did tackle him wished they hadn't. As Jack Youngblood, a former All-Pro defensive end for the Rams, put it, "He rattles your teeth."

The Chicago quarterback was Jim McMahon, who was the second-highest rated quarterback in the NFC behind Joe Montana. Jim was a fine passer and runner and the leader of the offense. As wide receiver Dennis McKinnon said, "It's just a different team when Jim's in there."

Matt Suhey, the fullback, was used mainly as a blocker for Payton, but he was a good runner, too (471 yards), and a fine pass receiver. The big-play receiver for the Bears was speedster Willie Gault, who caught 39 passes and led the NFC in average yards per catch (21.3). The offensive line, led by Pro-Bowlers Wally Hilgenberg at center and Jim Covert at tackle, provided tremendous blocking. The fact that the Bears led the league in rushing for three consecutive seasons is evidence of that fact. As Covert modestly said about their effort, "It's a pretty good accomplishment."

As good as the offense was, the defense was better—some people said it may have been the best defensive team ever. The Bears' defense played most of the time in a formation known as the 46 defense. It was devised by assistant coach Buddy Ryan, and basically, it puts a lot of pressure on an offense by bringing eight men up close to the line of scrimmage. The defense is designed to stop the run and pressure the passer. But even better than the system were the players.

Richard Dent, at right end, was a Pro-Bowler and had led the league in sacks the last two seasons (17½ in 1984 and 17 in 1985). Dan Hampton, another Pro-Bowler, was at left end and at the tackles were Steve McMichael and rookie sensation William ("The Refrigerator") Perry.

Middle linebacker Mike Singletary was another Pro-Bowler and, according to Coach Ditka, "He's the man who puts all the parts together." Joining him were outside linebackers Otis Wilson, a Pro-Bowler who had recorded 11 1/2 sacks during the season, and Wilbur Marshall, a top young player who hit hard.

The secondary was strong, with Leslie Frazier (a team-leading six interceptions) and Mike Richardson (four interceptions) at the corners, and Gary Fencik (a team-leading 118 tackles) and Dave Duerson, a Pro-Bowler, at the safety positions.

The Bears not only won; they also created a lot of controversy and curiosity in fans all across the country —especially McMahon and Perry.

McMahon, with his dark glasses, punk-rocker hairdo, and outspokenness, bothered a lot of people who have problems with individualists. Many other fans, though, welcomed his honesty and his humor.

When Refrigerator had reported to training camp weighing more than 300 pounds, defensive coach Buddy Ryan took a look at him and watched him work out. Then Ryan told reporters that the Bears had "wasted their first-round pick" on the bloated Mr. Perry. Perry, though, lost some weight, worked hard, and became a fine defensive tackle. But he really caught America's attention when Coach Ditka began using him in the offensive backfield when the Bears were near their opponent's goal line. TV fans all across the country—and around the world—were delighted by the sight of a 300-pounder crashing into the line either as a blocker or ball carrier.

During the season, The Fridge ran for two scores, caught a pass for another, and terrorized defenses when he bowled over defenders as the lead blocker.

The New England Patriots, with an 11-5 record, entered the play-offs as a wild-card team. They became the only team ever to win three consecutive play-off games on the road as they beat the Jets, 26-14, rapped the Raiders, 27-20, and mauled Miami, 31-14.

New England hadn't won in the Orange Bowl (Miami's home stadium) since 1966, the Dolphin's first season. They had lost there 18 consecutive times, including a 30–27 loss four weeks earlier. But the Pats really rocked them in the AFC title game as they intercepted Marino twice and recovered four fumbles. As Dolphin defensive end Doug Betters said after the game, "It was no mystery what they were going to do, we just couldn't stop them. They don't do any high-tech stuff; they just blow you off the ball."

They were coming into the Super Bowl on a real roll. Tony Eason, their young quarterback, had played especially well during the play-offs, and the veteran Steve Grogan was probably the best reserve quarterback in the league. He had even started six games during the season, and New England had won five of them (he had to leave the sixth after suffering a broken leg). The Pats had been the second-best rushing team in the AFC with 2,331 yards gained. Craig James was the leader with 1,227 yards and had become one of the best backs in the league. Fullback Tony Collins added 657 rushing yards and led the team with 52 receptions, good for another 549 yards. They had excellent speed at wide receiver in Stanley Morgan and Stephen Starring (playing for the injured Irving Fryar). A lot of football people thought they had the best offensive line in the game, especially on the left side, where tackle Brian Holloway and guard John Hannah were both Pro-Bowlers.

Their defense was strong and loaded with hitters. Andre Tippett, the left outside linebacker, was a Pro-Bowler, and, according to many experts, the best linebacker in the league during the season. He had led the AFC with 16 1/2 sacks. Don Blackman, the right outside linebacker, was also an excellent player who had the strength to stop the run and the speed to cover wide receivers. Raymond Clayborn, who had 6 interceptions, was a fine corner back as was free safety Fred Marion, who had 7 interceptions.

New England caught a break when they recovered a Walter Payton fumble on the second play of the game at the Chicago 19. But after three straight incomplete passes, they had to settle for a Tony Franklin field goal.

Chicago came right back to tie the game on a Kevin Butler field goal as they drove 59 yards in eight plays. The big play in the drive was a 43-yard pass from McMahon to Willie Gault.

The Patriots' second possession was much like the first: two incompletions and a punt. And their next possession was even worse: Craig James ran for no gain and then Richard Dent and Wilbur Marshall shared a sack on Eason. The double hit produced a fumble that Chicago recovered on the New England 13. They turned it into another Butler field goal after the Refrigerator was thrown for a 1-yard loss while trying to *throw* his first NFL pass.

On New England's first play after the kickoff, Dent jarred James with a terrific tackle, which separated James from the ball. The Bears recovered on the 13 and Matt Suhey ran for 2 yards and then 11 more for the first touchdown of the game, giving Chicago a 13-6 lead.

New England took the kickoff and ran one play before the end of the first quarter. They ran two more unsuccessful plays to start the second quarter, and then had to call on Rich Camarillo, who was, at least, getting some exercise punting the ball. The Bears took the punt and drove 59 yards in ten plays to up the score to 20-3. The big plays were an 8 yard run by reserve Dennis Gentry on a third-and-5 at the beginning of the drive and a 24-yard pass from McMahon to Matt Suhey. McMahon scored the TD on a 2-yard run.

Chicago soon got the ball back and drove 72 yards in 11 plays. McMahon again keyed the drive with a third-down toss to Gentry, a 29-yarder to Ken Margerum, and a 7-yard scramble to the 3-yard line. Butler kicked his third field goal on the last play of the half as the Bears took a 23-3 lead.

New England had been completely dominated. They had managed to gain only 19 yards, one first down, two pass completions, and three points. Midway through the second quarter, Coach Raymond Berry had replaced Eason with Grogan. "I was slightly shocked," Eason said about the onslaught of the Bears. "I couldn't understand it." Mike Singletary, though, understood it. "You could see it in his eyes very early. A look that said, 'Oh my, here we go again.'"

The Pats took the second-half kickoff and managed to eke out a first down before Grogan was sacked twice and they had to punt again (practice makes perfect). The punt pinned Chicago back at their own 4-yard line. McMahon called the signals, faked a handoff, and then set to throw from inside his own end zone. Helped by the fake, Gault flew past the defenders and caught a 60-yard pass from McMahon. Eight plays later, McMahon scored his second TD on a 1-yard run and Chicago led, 30-3.

The clock kept running, but the game was over right there. The Bears added 16 more points on an interception return by Reggie Phillips; a one-yard run by the Refrigerator that was set up by yet another interception by Chicago; and finally, a safety when Waechter tackled Grogan in the end zone. Oh, yes, New England scored in the fourth quarter on an eight-yard pass from Grogan to Fryar.

Before the game, Grogan had told reporters, "I had a dream before the season started that we'd be in the Super Bowl, and I'd come off the bench and be the hero." But, in reality, Grogan's dream turned into a nightmare, at least for New England.

There was great joy in the Chicago locker room. They had won by the largest margin in Super Bowl history and had kept the Pats to a Super Bowl record low of seven yards rushing! They also tied a Super Bowl record with seven sacks and recovered four fumbles and made two interceptions. It was awesome!

Richard Dent, who shared two sacks, forced two fumbles, and blocked a pass, was chosen the Most Valuable Player.

McMahon and Perry and the entire squad had enjoyed their Super Sunday. The only down note was that Walter Payton, in his first championship game after 11 seasons, didn't run for more yardage (66) or score a touchdown.

SUPER BOWL XXI

January 25, 1987

NEW YORK GIANTS
vs.
DENVER
"Bronco Busters"

THE GIANTS WON the NFC East with a 14-2 record, which tied the Bears for the best record in the league. Then the Giants slaughtered the 49ers, 49-3, and whitewashed Washington, 17-0, to earn a trip to the Rose Bowl and their first Super Bowl game.

The Giants finished the regular season with nine consecutive victories. They came into the play-offs red-hot, and after they thoroughly demolished a very strong 49er team and shut out a Washington team that was good enough to beat the Bears, they were on fire!

Their major threat on offense was Joe Morris, an explosive running back. Although opponents geared their defenses to stop him each game, he still managed to rush for a team record of 1,516 yards and score 14 touchdowns. He also caught 21 passes, which were good for 223 yards and another touchdown. Fullback Maurice Carthon, with only 260 yards gained, was their second-leading rusher, but his main value to the team was as a blocker. It was his blocking that frequently created the daylight for Morris to run through. As Joe modestly but accurately put it, "When Joe Morris has a great game, it is because Maurice Carthon has a great game."

Morris ran behind a very good offensive line that included Brad Benson, a Pro-Bowl selection at one tackle and Karl Nelson at the other, and guards Billy Ard and Chris Godfrey along with center Bart Oates.

Mark Bavaro, the Giants' All-Pro tight end, was also a valuable blocker as well as the team's leading receiver. He caught 66 passes for 1,005 yards and became only the seventh tight end in the history of the NFL to gain more than 1,000 yards in one season. Chicago coach Mike Ditka, who had been an All-Pro tight end himself, had this to say about Mark: "I think Bavaro is the best, the only true tight end in football. He blocks. He catches. He's a dominant player who challenges defenses."

The Giants didn't have an outstanding wide receiver, but they had a lot of effective ones. Lionel Manuel, just rounding into form after being out most of the season with an injury, was the most dangerous deep threat. Bobby Johnson, Stacey Robinson, and Phil McConkey (who also returned punts and kickoffs) made important contributions as did reserve tight end Zeke Mowatt.

The quarterback was Phil Simms. He had a strong arm and showed flashes of passing brilliance during the season when he threw for scores that resulted in last-minute victories. But he never seemed to put it together for long stretches.

On defense, the Giants were *awesome!* After giving up 31 points to Dallas in an opening game loss, only one other team had scored more than 20 points against them. And that only happened in the last game of the season when the Giants eased off in a game where they blew out Green Bay, 55-24. The heart of the defense was the linebackers—the best linebacking unit in the league, perhaps of all time. And the giant of the group was Lawrence Taylor. Big at 6'3" and 245 pounds and so fast that he could chase down running backs, Taylor terrorized offenses. Taylor usually lined up at the outside right position, but he often moved around to confuse offensive blocking patterns. As one football official put it, "When quarterbacks come out of the huddle, the first thing they do is look for where Number 56 is lined up." And no matter where he started, he usually wound up where the ball was, tackling a runner or sacking a quarterback. L. T. had led the league with 20 1/2 sacks and was selected as the NFL's Most Valuable Player, only the second defensive player ever to win the award!

Adding to opponents' problems was the emergence into stardom of the other outside linebacker, Carl Banks. He, too, was big and strong and fast, and no team had figured out a way to stop both of them. In the middle was the defensive captain and Pro-Bowler Harry Carson, and Gary Reasons.

The three starters on the line were also outstanding. Two of them, nose tackle Jim Burt and right end Leonard Marshall, were Pro-Bowl selections, and the third, left end George Martin, was a big play performer. The secondary was solid and got the job done.

The emphasis on the Giants was attack. They attacked on offense; they attacked on defense; they even attacked with their special teams. And they didn't quit. Twice during the season, they had been down by 17 points and had come back to win both games.

The Denver Broncos won the AFC West with an 11-5 record and then nipped New England, 22-17, and won a thriller over Cleveland, 23-20, in overtime.

In the Cleveland game, John Elway showed why most football experts had predicted superstardom for him. Denver had the ball on their own 2-yard line with less than six minutes left and down by a touchdown. But Elway led them down that cold and snowy field and with 39 seconds left, threw a 5-yard pass that tied the score. Then in the sudden-death overtime period, he hit on a 60-yard pass that set up Rich Karlis' winning field goal. Peak performance!

What made Elway such a threat was his great arm (which Kenny Hill of the Giants called "a cannon"), his ability to scramble, and either throw on the move or run for yardage (he was Denver's third-leading ground gainer and led all AFC quarterbacks in rushing for the third consecutive year). As Lawrence Taylor said before the game, "The biggest thing we have to do is take care of John Elway."

Sammy Winder was the leading rusher with 789 yards and 9 touchdowns and he also scored 5 touchdowns on pass receptions to give him the AFC lead with 14. Gerald Wilhite was their second-leading rusher and their top pass catcher with 64. Steve Watson was their leading wide receiver with 45 grabs.

Denver's defense was ranked first in the AFC against the run. Their best players were end Rulon Jones, a big strong pass rusher, and linebackers Tom Jackson and Karl Mecklenberg. (Denver used Mecklenberg all over the field the way the Giants used

L. T.) Maurice Carthon, the Giant fullback, said "He's just like L. T. is for us. He's a great player." They also had the best tackling secondary in the AFC.

Denver took the opening kickoff and on the very first play, Elway faked a handoff in one direction and then spun around and ran the opposite way for a 10-yard gain. Then he hit wide receiver Mark Jackson for 24 yards to bring the Broncos into Giant territory. The defense, though, dug in and Denver had to settle for a 3-0 lead on a Rich Karlis field goal.

The Giants took the kickoff and stormed right back. Simms hit Manuel for 17 yards and Morris ran for 11. Then Simms threw to Robinson for 18 and Bavaro for 9. Simms completed the nine-play, 78-yard drive with a 6-yard pass to Zeke Mowatt and the Giants led, 7-3.

Ken Bell took Raul Allegre's kickoff and gave Denver excellent field position by running it back to the Bronco's 42-yard line. Elway had a party as he hit Winder for 14, Mobley for 11, and Winder again for 9 to put the ball inside the Giant 30. Two penalties against the Giants moved the ball inside the 10 and three plays later, Elway lugged it in from the 4 to give Denver a 10-7 lead.

The first time the Broncos had the ball in the second period, Elway went back to pass from his own 18. The Giant rush forced John to scramble out of the pocket, but he bought the time he needed to pick out a receiver, and hit Vance Johnson with a bull's-eye inside the Giant 30. Denver kept driving until they had a first down and goal to go from the 1. They were primed to build a big lead and put serious pressure on the Giants. Elway tried a pass-run option on first down but L. T. knifed in and dropped him for a 1-yard loss. Willhite tried to run up the middle on second down but he ran into a brick wall named Harry Carson for no gain. On third down, Elway pitched out to Winder but Carl Banks cut into the Bronco backfield and dropped him for a four-yard loss. The Broncos had run three plays and *lost* 5 yards! Karlis came in to salvage a field goal out of the stalled drive, but he missed the 23-yarder—the shortest miss in Super Bowl history—and Denver came up empty.

After the Giants punted, their defense took charge again as George Martin and Erik Howard sacked Elway in the end zone. The 2-point safety cut Denver's lead to 10-9.

Late in the second quarter, Elway struck again. He hit Watson with a 31-yard toss inside the Giant 35, and then hit Willhite at the 20. But again the defense stiffened and forced three incompletions. Karlis came in to attempt another field goal but missed *again*, this time from 34 yards out.

During half time, Coach Bill Parcells told the Giants that while they had made some big plays, they weren't being consistent. "You're running around wild. We have to play with more discipline. Don't *give* it away."

The Giants took the opening kickoff and were stopped short of a first down on their opening series. The punting teams took the field but Coach Parcells had decided to try a trick play. Jeff Rutledge, the Giants' backup quarterback, ducked in behind the center, took the snap, and ran to the Giant 48 for a first down before the startled Broncos could recover. Given a second chance, the Giants' offense quickly cashed in. On first down, Simms hit Morris for 12 and on the next play, he hit reserve running back Lee Rouson for 23 more. After two running plays, Simms hit his third consecutive pass on the drive, a 13-yard TD toss to Bavaro. When asked afterward why he had taken the gamble, Parcells replied, "We came here to win." The Giants had a 16-10 lead and it was their time to party.

After the kickoff, Denver ran three plays and then was forced to punt. McConkey took the kick at the Giants' 43 and ripped off a 25-yard return, down to the Bronco 32. The Giant drive was stopped inside the 10, but Allegre came in and kicked a 21-yard field goal to up their lead to 19-10.

Denver took the kickoff but again the Giant defense allowed them only three plays and a punt. And once again, the Giants struck quickly. First Simms tossed to Manuel for 17 yards. Next he handed off to Morris, who faked into the line and then spun around and pitched the ball *back* to Simms. The defense had been fooled by the flea-flicker and Simms threw a perfect pass to McConkey, who was all alone at the 20. McConkey ran it down to the 1 before he was tackled. Behind a crunching block by Bavaro, Joe Morris ran it in to give the Giants a 26-10 lead with less than nine minutes left in the third quarter. The Giants were breaking out the party hats.

Elvis Patterson intercepted Elway's first pass of the fourth period, and Simms was on the prowl again with a first down at the Giant 48. He tossed 36 yards to Robinson and two plays later, threw a 6 yard touchdown that bounced off Bavaro's fingers, but right into the waiting hands of the ever-present McConkey. The Giants led, 33-10, and Harry Carson was eyeing the Gatorade.

Denver took the kickoff and finally mounted a drive after having been completely shut down in the third period. They moved 74 yards in 13 plays, but had to settle for a field goal when the drive was stopped at the Giants' 10-yard line.

And the Giants were *still* partying! Rouson ran for

18 yards and then Simms ripped off a 22-yarder. O. J. Anderson took it in the last 2 yards and the Giants led, 39-13 (the extra point was missed).

Denver scored another touchdown to cut the final score to 39-20, but the victory party was for the Giants. And they celebrated in their usual style when Harry Carson sneaked up behind Coach Bill Parcells and doused him with a vat full of Gatorade.

Phil Simms set an all-time record for passing—not just for the Super Bowl, but for all post-season games ever played in the NFL!—by hitting for an amazing 22 of 25. He had played a great game, or as Giant offense coach Ron Erhardt called it, "a perfect game." And Phil was rewarded with the MVP award and a dousing by teammates Brad Benson and Bert Oates. Said Oates, "I think it was very appropriate to cool the guy down, as hot as he was in the game."

SUPER BOWL XXII

January 31, 1988

DENVER vs. WASHINGTON

"*Perfection*"

DENVER WAS BACK for its second consecutive appearance, and this year they were determined to prevail. "We want to win the Super Bowl this time," said John Elway. "As much as we talked about not being happy just to be there last year, I think deep down we were. This year, we want to win it because we know what it's like to lose. Losing to the Giants has stuck with us all year."

Denver's first step on the road to Jack Murphy Stadium in San Diego was to win the AFC Western Division title, which they accomplished with a 10-4-1 record in a strike-shortened season. Then they went on to humble Houston 34-10, which set up a rematch with the Cleveland Browns for the AFC championship.

For the second consecutive year the Broncos and the Browns staged one of the most memorable play-off games ever played. Once again John Elway and Bernie Kosar hooked up in a duel that forever linked their careers and that kept millions of viewers on the edge of their seats.

Elway led the Broncos to a 21-3 halftime lead, but Kosar rallied the Browns with 3 second-half TD passes to tie the game at 31-31 late in the fourth quarter. Elway responded to that challenge by leading Denver on a long drive, which he capped with a 20-yard scoring toss to Sammy Winder with only 4:01 left in the game. Kosar, though, brought the Browns right back with a brilliant drive and had them headed in for the tying score when lightning struck in the person of Jeremiah Castille. Castille stripped the ball from running back Ernest Byner and recovered it on the 2-yard line with only 1:05 left to play.

"I'm enjoying it now that it's over," said a happy John Elway about the 38-33 victory. "But it was a little nerve-wracking at the time.'

The Washington Redskins dethroned the Super Bowl champion Giants to capture the NFC Eastern Division title with an 11-4 record. Then they beat a tough Bears team when All-Pro cornerback Darrell Green broke off a dazzling 52-yard punt return to supply the winning points in a 21-17 win. Their opponent in the championship game was the surprising Minnesota Vikings, who had sneaked into the play-offs with an 8-7 record. The Vikes had advanced to the game by smashing the Saints, who had been 12-3 during the season, 44-10, and by flattening the 49ers, 36-24. In successive weeks the team with the worst record in the play-offs had eliminated the teams with the two best regular season records.

Washington finally put a stop to this string of upsets

as they won a 17-10 nail-biter. The Redskins took the lead with 5:15 left in the fourth quarter when Doug Williams smoked a TD pass to Gary Clark. And they just managed to avoid OT when Darrin Nelson dropped a short pass at the goal line with 56 seconds left in the game.

Denver was favored to win the Super Bowl for one reason—John Elway. Elway had been selected as the NFL's MVP by the Associated Press and as the starting quarterback for the AFC in the Pro Bowl. Around the league most people thought that he was the best quarterback playing, maybe the best of all time. Sid Gillman, a great veteran coach, said it flat out. "I've never seen a guy who can beat you in so many ways. I've never seen anyone like Elway."

Tom Landry, the resident genius of the Dallas Cowboys, defined Washington's problem. "In figuring a way to stop the Broncos, you start with containing Elway from the outside with your defensive ends. The problem is, nobody ever does."

Teams usually attempt to flush quarterbacks out of the pocket, outside of their protective shell of blockers. But teams don't want to do that with John because that's exactly when he's at his most dangerous, when he's on the loose, behind the line of scrimmage, twisting and turning away from his pursuers, able to take off downfield himself or to buy time for the defense to break down and his receivers to break free.

Hanford Dixon, a Pro-Bowl cornerback for Cleveland, spoke with awe about John's ability to strike. "I never saw another quarterback run to one side of the field and throw the ball to the opposite side like he does. His arm is so strong that he doesn't give you much recovery time if you're off your receiver. That's what sets him apart from all other quarterbacks."

Even people who picked Washington always acknowledged the "Elway Factor," as though he was a force of nature that could erupt at any time and wreak total havoc. As Kellon Winslow, the tight end of the Chargers, put it, "I'll pick Washington. They have bigger offensive and defensive lines and they'll dominate. *But* they have to keep Elway off the field."

The Washington players and coaching staff were also aware of the danger that Elway represented. Dexter Manley, their hard-charging defensive end, put it very bluntly. "If we don't stop Elway, we'll lose. You can take it to the bank and cash it. He's magic, a one-man show. He can be stopped; he's not Superman, but you have to be relentless."

Joe Gibbs, the 'Skins' head coach, was concerned about Elway's improvisational talents, his ability to scramble and create a play that was never designed—that is, therefore, impossible to prepare for. "You don't know what he's going to do. It's like a time bomb. It's going to go off—you just don't know when."

And what does the subject of all this talk and concern think about his freewheeling style? "It's fun. It's like playing in the street. Everybody is just trying to find room to get open. It's total chaos. Yeah, I enjoy that."

Doug Williams, the "other" quarterback, had taken a circuitous route to San Diego. He had begun his career as the number one draft pick of Tampa Bay. After five unhappy and uneven years with the Buccaneers, he sat out a year and then signed with the Oklahoma Outlaws of the USFL. When that league folded, Doug was out of a job until he got a call from Joe Gibbs to come to Washington to back up Jay Schroeder. Doug spent the 1986 season and much of the 1987 season warming the bench, not getting a chance to play until injury and ineffectiveness gave him his golden opportunity.

The question most often asked of Williams was how it felt to be the first black quarterback ever to play in a Super Bowl. Doug, who is a fierce competitor but a very gentle human being, was nevertheless annoyed at the question. "I'm not some kind of experiment. I'm a good quarterback. And I got a bunch of guys—white and black—protecting my case. I don't think Joe Jacoby or Mark May think of me as black or white. They think of me as their quarterback.

"Joe Gibbs and [General Manager] Bobby Beathard didn't bring me in to be the first black quarterback in the Super Bowl. They brought me in to be the quarterback of the Washington Redskins."

The time bomb that Gibbs had feared exploded in Washington's secondary the very first time that Elway touched the ball in Super Bowl XXII. On Denver's first play from scrimmage he threw a 56-yard strike to Ricky Nattiel, who had flown right past a stunned Barry Wilburn, and faster than you could light a fuse the Broncos led 7-0. The score by Nattiel, one of the trio of wide receivers known collectively as "The Three Amigos," came with only 1:57 gone in the game, the fastest TD ever scored in a Super Bowl.

On Denver's next possession Elway smoked a 32-yard completion to Mark Jackson, another Amigo, and then *caught* a 23-yard pass from halfback Steve Sewell deep in Washington territory. It was the first pass ever caught by a quarterback in a Super Bowl game. The drive was halted inside Washington's 10-yard line when Dave Butz stopped John on a quarterback draw, but Rich Karlis kicked a field goal and the Broncos led 10-0. It looked like it might be a blowout.

When Denver got the ball back, they drove down to Washington's 30-yard line, but they came away empty when strong safety Alvin Walton sacked Elway for an 18-yard loss and pushed the Broncos out of field-goal range.

When the first quarter came to an end, Denver was clearly the dominant team. They were executing their offense, and their defense, helped by four dropped passes by Washington receivers, had shut down the 'Skins' offense. Denver had outgained Washington 142 yards to 63, and more importantly, they led 10-0. No team in Super Bowl history had ever come back from a 10-point deficit.

And then, suddenly, like a summer storm breaking from a cloudless sky, the Redskins burst all over the Broncos. On their first offensive play of the second quarter, from their own 20-yard line, Williams play-faked in the backfield while wide receiver Ricky Sanders flew past Denver cornerback Mark Haynes, who had tried to jam him at the line of scrin 1age. Williams threw a perfect pass, and in one 80-y rd play Washington was back in the game. As Washington defensive end Charles Mann said, "Momentum is something you can't touch, feel, or see, but it was there once Ricky Sanders scored."

Washington quickly got the ball back and moved to Denver's 27. On third and one, with everyone expecting a run, Williams crossed up the Broncos and threw a perfect lead pass to a diving Gary Clark to give the 'Skins a 14-10 lead. On their next possession Washington again struck with snakelike swiftness. Williams hit Clark over the middle for 16 yards. And then Timmy Smith, a rookie in his first NFL start, ripped off a 56-yard TD romp that upped their lead to 21-10.

Denver was demoralized. "Their touchdowns kept coming so quickly," said Denver linebacker Jim Ryan, "that it just robbed us of the opportunity to do anything about it. After the first one, you try to shrug it off. After the second one, you get a little frustrated, and I'm sure that it went through a lot of guys' minds, 'Here we go again.' After the third one, you're in a whirlpool and you're sinking."

And Washington wasn't about to throw them a life preserver. On their next possession Williams threw a 50-yard scoring pass to Sanders, and Washington stretched its lead to 28-10. Elway tried to rally Denver, but Barry Wilburn, who had been beaten earlier on Nattiel's TD, burned the Broncos by intercepting a pass at Washington's 21-yard line. Williams moved the 'Skins' offense with the precision of a Swiss watch. He connected with Sanders twice, and then Smith exploded for a 43-yard run. One a third and four from the 8-yard line, with Denver's defense completely demoralized, Williams calmly hit tight end Clint Didier for Washington's fifth consecutive touchdown and a 35-10 lead.

A few plays later Washington completed the most spectacular quarter in Super Bowl history. They had set a sackful of Super Bowl records, including 35 points and 356 yards of offense in one unforgettable quarter. Sanders caught 5 passes for 168 yards and 2 TD's, Smith rushed 5 times for 122 yards, including a 58-yard TD burst, and Williams completed 9 of 11 passes for 228 yards and 4 TD's. They had played the perfect quarter.

Defensively, Washington neutralized Elway as their front four plugged up his scrambling lanes; the defensive backs blanketed the receivers, and strong safety Alvin Walton shadowed Elway's every move. "They were just hanging him in the middle," Elway noted. "If I started to move, he was running after me. If I didn't, he dropped into pass coverage."

They played the second half just to make the game official and to see who would win the MVP award—

Williams, Smith, or Sanders. Along the way, Smith ran for another TD to make the final score 42-10, the fourth consecutive Super Bowl win for the NFC.

Elway, who was held to 14 completions in 38 attempts and suffered 3 interceptions and 5 sacks, showed his class after the game by answering reporters' questions for more than half an hour and by refusing to alibi. "We just never answered the bell in the second quarter. It's the same way we felt last year. We know how to get here, but we've got to figure out a way to win one."

In the other locker room a jubilant Joe Gibbs admitted, "I was shocked we played as well as we did. It was the best I've ever seen a Washington team play." How well they played can be judged by some of the records that they set as a team, including most yards rushing (280) and most total yards (602), and by some of the individual records that they set, including most yards rushing—Timmy Smith, 204 (the previous record was 191 by Marcus Allen with the Raiders in 1984); most yards receiving—Ricky Sanders, 193 (the previous record was 161 by Lynn Swann with the Steelers, 1976); and most yards passing—Doug Williams, 340 (the previous record was 331, Joe Montana, 49ers, 1985).

Williams, who had spent three hours in a dentist's chair the day before and had sat out Washington's last two offensive plays in the first quarter with a hyperflexed left knee, was named the MVP. Gary Clark expressed the admiration of all his teammates when he said, "The guy was in pain all game. But what a performance. He saved his best for the best."

SUPER BOWL XXIII

January 22, 1989

SAN FRANCISCO
vs.
CINCINNATI

"The Team of the '80s"

AFTER SURGING TO win the NFL Western Division with a 10-6 record and then going on to rout the Vikings, 34-9, and the Bears, 28-3, the San Francisco 49ers were back in the Super Bowl for the third time, going for the win that would establish them as the team of the '80s.

It had been a long, uphill climb for the team and its veteran quarterback, Joe Montana. With only five games to go in the regular season, the 49ers had found themselves floundering in third place in the division—struggling along with a 6-5 record and facing the possibility of not making the play-offs. But the Montana-led 49ers had responded to the challenge like champions by winning their next four games.

But despite the stirring stretch drive that had put them in the play-off picture for a sixth straight season, the

49ers' recent history in postseason play didn't provide their fans with much promise of continued success.

The 49ers had been eliminated in the opening round in each of the last three years, and their losses had been highlighted by the failure of their three offensive super-stars—quarterback Joe Montana, runningback Roger Craig, and wide receiver Jerry Rice—to produce a single touchdown in those three games.

But the 49ers and their trio of superstars shook off the ghosts of those past performances in their play-off rout of the Vikings. Montana hooked up with Rice for three first-half TD tosses, and Craig closed out the scoring with two fourth-quarter scores, including an 80-yard romp, the longest run from scrimmage in NFL post-season history. After the game Montana expressed the entire team's feelings of relief and satisfaction when he said, "It's been a long road to get here. There's been a lot of pressure on us for not winning the last few years in the first round."

The 49ers had cleared another roadblock on their way to Joe Robbie Stadium and the warm weather of Miami, but their road to the Super Bowl first had to pass through the chilling cold of Chicago, where the Bears, the Prae-torian guards of Soldier Field, stood waiting.

At game time a winter weather pattern sent arctic winds whipping across Lake Michigan, creating a wind-chill factor of minus 26 degrees. But the 49ers refused to bend to the Bears or the weather. On their third possession Montana defied the numbing cold and swirl-ing winds and fired a 20-yard pass toward Rice, who had run an out pattern to the right side of the field. The gifted receiver beat the cornerback to the inside, snared the ball at the top of his leap, juked out a second de-fender, and galloped the last 40 yards into the end zone to complete a scintillating 61-yard play that gave the 49ers a 7-0 lead.

Montana and Rice hooked up for another score in the second quarter, after strong safety Jeff Fuller intercepted a poorly thrown pass by Jim McMahon. And in the third quarter Montana put the Bears on the ropes when he connected with tight end John Frank for his third touchdown toss of the day. The 49ers' fullback, Tom Rathman, delivered the knockout blow, busting up the middle and into the end zone to put the finishing touch on a thoroughly awesome performance. As Dan Hampton, the Bears' straight-talking Pro Bowl defensive tackle, put it, "The 49ers controlled the game from the git-go. They kicked our butt. Anybody tries to tell you anything else, they're a liar."

Bill Walsh, the 49ers tight-lipped coach, was ecstatic. "This is as great a game as we've had in many, many years. We've played back-to-back great football games." And then he put his arm around his quarterback's shoulder and said, "It's one of the greatest games Joe Montana has ever played."

Walsh's words were sweet music to Montana, who had suffered through a year of playing musical chairs with Steve Young for the starting-quarterback spot. Joe had been benched twice and had his confidence severely shaken by Walsh's earlier lack of faith. "By far, this was my toughest season," said Joe—even worse than 1986, when he had undergone serious back surgery and missed much of the season. "This year I felt like I was trying to be counted out, and I didn't understand it. I felt like I had a good training camp, threw the ball well, and yet there seemed to be that constant feeling that if I had a bad game, a few bad series, that Steve would be in there. I haven't reached a comfort zone where I feel the job is mine.''

It had been a long, tough trip, but Joe had stuck it out, rallying the 49ers in their stretch run and leading them through the play-offs and on to Miami.

The Cincinnati Bengals were also a team on the rebound. The year before, dissension had ripped the team apart as the head coach, Sam Wyche, and the quarterback, Boomer Esiason, had openly feuded. After the Bengals finished the season with a 4-11 record, a lot of people in the Queen City would have been happy to see both of them leave town. But prior to the start of the 1988 season, Boomer and Wyche reconciled their differences, and the Bengals went on to become the surprise winners of the AFC Central Division with a conference-best 12-4 record. Then they went on to stop the Seattle Seahawks, 21-13, and beat the Buffalo Bills, 21-10, in the AFC championship game.

Boomer Esiason's left-handed passes had propelled the Bengals early in the season, and he did it well enough to finish the season as the NFL's top-rated quarterback and the league's MVP. Later in the season, when Wyche decided to emphasize the running game, rookie running back Ickey Woods burst upon the scene. Woods, a big, bruising back, was the Bengals' leading rusher, with 1,066 yards and 15 TDs. Woods gained the media spotlight and national fame for the ''Ickey Shuffle,'' a little dance routine that he did to celebrate his touchdowns.

James Brooks, a nondancing but multitalented running back, also made a major contribution, totaling 14 touchdowns while running for 931 yards and snaring 29 passes.

Up front, moving the bodies, was a huge and talented line. Many football people, including Buffalo's Pro Bowl nose tackle, Fred Smerlas, who had seen it up close and personal, considered it to be the NFL's best offensive line.

The best of the best, and the *smallest* player on the line at six feet six and 278 pounds, was Anthony Munoz. Munoz, a Pro Bowl selection for eight consecutive years, was voted the NFL's 1988 offensive lineman of the year. On the right side veteran guard Max Montoya had not allowed a *single* sack in 1988.

All that talent working together had made the Bengals the top rushing team and the number-one offense in the NFL. And the Bengals defense, which had been only mediocre during the season, had turned into tigers in postseason play, totally disrupting their opponents' offenses and limiting them to a combined 23 points.

Tim Krumrie, the nose tackle whom Seattle coach Chuck Knox had dubbed the best in the NFL, anchored the defensive line. The backfield, manned by safeties David Fulcher and Solomon Wilcots and cornerbacks Lewis Billups and Eric Thomas, was young, hard hitting, and cocky. They called themselves "The Swat Team," and their nickname matched their style of play.

Both San Francisco and Cincinnati had come a long way and overcome a lot of obstacles, but now that the two teams had reached the Super Bowl, most of the experts were predicting that the 49ers would blow the Bengals away. When Wyche was asked how the team felt about being buried before the game had begun, he quipped, "Our team took a vote, and we plan to show up for all four quarters." But there were solid reasons to believe that the 49ers would win convincingly. They had closed the season with a rush and then lifted their game to an even higher level during the play-offs.

The defense, led by free safety and perennial Pro Bowler Ronnie Lott, strong safety Jeff Fuller, nose tackle Michael Carter, and monster man Charles Haley, had ranked third best in the NFL during the season, but in the postseason they had turned the vise even tighter. And their three game-breakers—Montana, Rice, and Craig—had hit new highs. Montana knew how to win the big games. He had been to the Super Bowl twice, and both times he had walked away with the winner's ring and the MVP trophy. As wide receiver Mike Wilson pointed out, "Joe has poise and control on the field. He's always been calm, cool Joe. He's the best."

And on the 49ers' second Super Bowl possession, Joe showed his cool and his skills. Masterfully mixing running plays with a short passing game, Montana led the 49ers 73 yards, from the shadow of their goal line to the Bengals' 24-yard line. But two dropped passes, including one by Mike Wilson at the two-yard line that had the instant-replay crew working overtime, stopped the drive, and the 49ers had to settle for three points on a 41-yard field goal by Mike Cofer.

On San Francisco's next possession Montana threw a 15-yard sideline pass toward Rice, who electrified the crowd by first tipping the ball and then making an incredible one-handed catch just before stepping out of bounds at the 49er 45. After Craig had given the 49ers another first down at the Bengal 42, Montana caught Lewis Billups trying to cover Rice one on one and made him pay the price by connecting with Rice for another first down at the ten-yard line. Faced with a fourth down after David Fulcher had made a touchdown-saving tackle at the two, Walsh decided to play conservatively and go for the 19-yard field goal. But Randy Cross's poor snap threw off the timing and caused Cofer to drill a line drive low and off to the left, the shortest miss in Super Bowl history.

On the very next series the Bengals were forced to punt after Ronnie Lott popped wide receiver Eddie Brown and dropped him just short of a first down. John Taylor, the 49ers' Pro Bowl punt-return specialist, misplayed the kick, and the ball took a Bengals' bounce behind Taylor all the way down to the 49ers' nine-yard line, for a Super Bowl record 63-yard punt. But Taylor raced back, scooped up the ball near the right sideline, broke a tackle, and picked up blockers as he raced across the field, running it back 45 yards to set yet another Super Bowl record. A normally routine punt had turned into a crowd-raising double record setter.

The 49ers, though, were unable to capitalize on the bizarre turn of events and their excellent field position because David Fulcher forced a fumble when he leveled Roger Craig in the open field with a thunderous shoulder smash while Roger was high-stepping his way toward a first down deep in Cincinnati territory.

But the Bengals offense, which had been sputtering throughout the first half, was unable to take advantage of the turnover. On their next possession, though, they parlayed favorable field position and an 18-yard completion into a 34-yard field goal by Jim Breech with 1:15 left in the half. The teams went into their locker rooms tied at 3-3, the first halftime tie in Super Bowl history and the lowest halftime score since the Steelers had a 2-0 lead in Super Bowl IX.

The teams had failed to produce the high-scoring fireworks that most people expected. The 49ers had moved the ball effectively early but had not cashed in on their opportunities, while the Bengals' running game had been neutralized by Boomer Esiason's poor passing. The supposedly sleek offenses were running more like back-yard lawn mowers than high-performance machines.

Boomer temporarily regained his touch on the opening drive of the second half as he passed the Bengals deep down the field. The drive stalled, though, and Breech had to come on to get a 43-yard field goal. But on the Bengals' very next possession, Boomer gave it right back by floating a pass that was picked off by rookie linebacker Bill Romanowski deep in Bengals' territory. The Bengals' defense rose to the occasion, though, and the 49ers were forced to settle for a Cofer field goal that tied the score at 6-6.

With less than a minute to play in the third quarter, neither team had dented the end zone. But Stanford Jennings took matters into his own hands when he took Cofer's kickoff at his own seven-yard line, ran straight up the middle behind a wedge of blockers, and burst out of the pack and into the clear for an electrifying 93-yard touchdown gallop that gave the Bengals a 13-6 lead.

But before the Bengals had a chance to build any momentum, Montana got the points back with three quick strikes. First he hit Rice with a short pass, which Rice turned into a 31-yard gain. Then on the first play of the fourth quarter, Montana connected with Craig for 40 yards down to the Bengal 14. Two plays later Rice caught a Montana pass at the five and somehow managed to hook the ball over the goal line as he was being pushed out of bounds by cornerback Lewis Billups.

With the score tied 13-13 and time running out, Boomer took the Bengals on a long drive that positioned

Breech's 40-yard field goal and gave Cincinnati a 16-13 lead with only 3:20 left in the game. Boomer and some of the other Bengals were starting to taste the win. "I figured, with the way our defense was playing, it was going to be a sweet ride home."

But Joe Montana and the 49ers had their own idea about how to end the game. With the ball at the eight-yard line after the kickoff, Montana came into the huddle and, according to tackle Bubba Paris, "When you looked in his eyes, you could almost see the Super Bowl ring on his finger." Knowing that the Bengals expected him to go to the sidelines, Montana began the drive by going over the middle first to Craig and then to tight end John Frank. After a short pass to Rice and two short bursts up the middle by Craig kept the drive alive, Montana, working without a huddle, lobbed a sideline pass to Rice at the Bengal 48 and then went over the middle to Craig at the 36. After a penalty moved the ball back to the Bengal 45, Montana threw his only incomplete pass of the drive. There was only 1:15 left in the game. Joe, though, stayed cool and went over the middle to Rice down to the 18 and then to Craig at the ten. With the clock ticking down, Montana dropped back, saw the double coverages on Rice and Craig, saw John Taylor streaking into the end zone, and threw a spiral into Taylor's outstretched hands with 34 seconds showing on the clock to give the 49ers a thrilling 20-16 win.

The 49ers, led by Jerry Rice and Joe Montana, had reached the top of the mountain. Rice, who was named the game's MVP, put on a spectacular show. His 11 receptions tied one Super Bowl record, and his 215 receiving yards broke the record set by Ricky Sanders in Super Bowl XXII. Jerry, who had been taunted all

—144—

week by the Bengals' defensive backs, had refused to get into a war of words before the game. And now that it was over, he just smiled and said, "I don't talk a game, I just go out and play it."

Montana had also come to play, passing for a Super bowl record 357 yards and directing one of the greatest drives of all times. As Boomer Esiason said, comparing the 49ers' last-minute win with Denver's win in the 1986 AFC championship game, "After what Joe did at the end, you might as well forget about that great Denver drive that got them into the Super Bowl. It's now the great San Francisco drive that *won* the Super Bowl. That indicates how great Joe Montana is." But the Bengals' veteran wide receiver Cris Collingsworth had the last word. "Joe Montana," he said with emphasis, "is not human."

SUPER BOWL XXIV

January 28, 1990

SAN FRANCISCO
vs.
DENVER
"The Big Easy"

WHILE THE 49ERS were still celebrating their thrilling victory in Super Bowl XXIII, Joe Montana had held the game ball above his head and, over the happy shouts and laughter of his teammates, pointed the 49ers toward the Louisiana Superdome and Super Bowl XXIV. "We're coming back," he announced. "We're going to repeat."

The 49ers, not satisfied with having been the team of the '80s, wanted to establish themselves as a team for the ages. And they knew that, to accomplish that goal, they would have to win back-to-back championships the way the great Pittsburgh Steeler and Miami Dolphin teams had done in the seventies, and the Green Bay Packers had done a decade earlier.

But before the 49ers could begin earning a trip to New Orleans, the city known as "The Big Easy," they first had to overcome the challenge of a head-coaching change. Bill Walsh, who had guided the team to its three Super Bowl wins, resigned, and George Seifert, who had been the 49ers' defensive co-ordinator for nine years, stepped up to the top spot.

The changeover caused the 49ers' offense to start the 1989 season out of sync, as Seifert retooled the line and offensive coordinator Mike Holmgren opened up the attack so that defenses couldn't consistently double team wide receiver Jerry Rice and running back Roger Craig without paying a price.

But the line changes paid off eventually, and Holmgren's strategy of spreading the ball around provided big dividends as the 49ers wound up as the top offensive unit in the NFL. Wide receiver John Taylor, given the chance to emerge from the giant shadow of Jerry Rice, responded by pulling down 60 receptions for over 1,000 yards and ten touchdowns. Fullback Tom Rathman also stepped forward, hauling in 73 passes, tops among NFL running backs. And sharing the wealth didn't put a dent in Rice's All-Pro numbers, which showed 82 catches good for almost 1,500 yards and a league-leading 17 TD's. And it didn't put a lid on Craig either, as he churned out over 1,000 yards rushing and almost 500 more on 49 receptions. And all Joe Montana did was have his best year yet while achieving the highest quarterback rating in the history of the NFL.

And although it was the 49ers' offense that usually drew the raves, their defense was just as devastating. And the heart and soul of the defense was their All-Pro free safety, Ronnie Lott. Lott, who led the 49ers with five interceptions and was called "our Joe Montana on defense" by coach Seifert, was paid the ultimate compliment by Denver's strong safety, Dennis Smith. "He's the best, the defensive back that everybody ranks their play by. He's the Michael Jordan of defensive backs."

So once the 49ers smoothed out the rough spots on offense, they cut through their NFL schedule like a high-speed hydrofoil, compiling a league-best 14–2 record.

Their first-round opponent in the play-offs was the Minnesota Vikings, the preseason pick to win the Super Bowl. The Vikings had the league's top-rated defense, and the ability to strike through the air and on the ground on offense. And the Vikes did draw first blood, marching 70 yards before settling for a field goal and a 3–0 lead. But then the deluge struck, and the Vikings were washed away in a torrent of 49er touchdowns.

On the first play from scrimmage after the field goal, Montana hit Rice on a short slant in, but Jerry put on the afterburners and turned the play into a 72-yard TD. And that play turned the game around, according to the Vikings' defensive coordinator, Floyd Peters. "The defense went into shock after that. It was a total collapse."

And Montana and company made sure they didn't recover. Before the half was over, "Joe Cool" had connected on three short scoring passes: the first to tight end Brent Jones; the second to John Taylor, which was set up by an interception and 28-yard runback by strong safety Chet Brooks; and the third to Rice on a 13-yard post pattern for his second score of the game.

And the 49ers kept the pressure on in the second half, too, completing a 41–13 rout over a frustrated and demoralized Vikings team. "We couldn't stop anything they did," said Keith Millard, the Vikings' All-Pro defensive tackle. "They score any time they want to. They won't be beaten the rest of the year."

The next test for the 49ers was the Los Angeles Rams in the NFC title game. The Rams had split their two games with the 49ers during the season and were coming off two rough play-off wins over two of the NFC's toughest teams, the Philadelphia Eagles and the New York Giants. The Rams players came into the game cocky, confident that they were the team to knock the 49ers off their lofty perch. "I think we're the only team in the league that can beat them," said wide receiver Flipper Anderson.

The Rams did manage to take an early 3–0 lead, and they even had the chance to go up 10–0 and just maybe take control of the game. But Ronnie Lott raced across the field and, at the last instant, deflected a Jim Everett pass away from Flipper Anderson's outstretched fingers. "He came out of nowhere," said a disbelieving Anderson. "An unbelievable play," marveled Ernie Zampese, the Rams' defensive coordinator.

The 49ers' defense kept the vise tight for the rest of the game, never allowing the Rams to reach their 40-yard line. And after surviving a shaky start, the only thing that stopped the 49ers' offense was the halftime whistle. But by then the 49ers led 21–3 and were safely on their way to a surprisingly easy 30–3 win.

Montana, operating behind an offensive line that gave him time to scan for secondary receivers, was magnificent. He connected on 26 of 30 passes to seven different receivers, including TD tosses to Brent Jones and John Taylor. The 18-yarder to Taylor, coming in the closing seconds of the first half, was the backbreaker. "That drive sent us reeling," said Rams' cornerback LeRoy Irwin. "We were on our heels the rest of the game."

In the 49ers' locker room, tackle Steve Wallace was whooping it up about the team's chance to win consecutive championships. "We want to be like Rudolph the Red-Nosed Reindeer. We want to go down in history." Roger Craig, though, already had his game face on. "It's money time. It's time to go to the Super Bowl. We can cherish this twenty years from now if we win. I want to be mentioned in the same breath as the Pittsburgh Steelers, Miami Dolphins, and Green Bay Packers."

And George Seifert, the 49ers' rookie head coach, spoke about the mission that fueled the 49ers' trip to New Orleans. "Of all the things we've accomplished here, back-to-back championships is something we haven't. I think that's been kind of a quiet battle cry for our players all season long."

The Denver Broncos didn't begin their season with *any* great expectations. Head coach Dan Reeves, reacting to the team's 8–8 record in 1988, had instituted a major retooling program in hopes of getting the team back to its winning ways. Reeves brought in Wade Phillips as the team's defensive coordinator, and Phillips recast and reschooled that unit so well that Denver became one of the top defensive teams in the NFL. The most important addition was free safety Steve Atwater, a hard-hitting, ball-hawking rookie who teamed with veteran strong safety Dennis Smith to give the Broncos a security blanket in their defensive backfield.

Reeves also revamped the offensive unit, adding five new starters, including rookie halfback Bobby Humphrey. Humphrey's running had given Denver a dynamic new dimension, adding balance to an attack that, for too long, had relied too heavily on John Elway's strong right arm.

The Denver coaching staff did a super job in meshing their ten new starters into the lineup, and the rebuilt Broncos broke quickly out of the starting blocks. They won ten of their first twelve games, becoming the first team in the league to qualify for the playoffs. But they dropped three of their last four games to close the season at 11–5, and then narrowly missed carrying their losing ways into their play-off game against the Pittsburgh Steelers. But just when it seemed that Denver's magic-carpet ride was going to crash, Reeves rubbed his Aladdin's lamp and out came John Elway.

Elway's play during the season had been inconsistent and disappointing, and he was forced to suffer through a trying time. Elway had been blasted by the media in Denver and had heard boos and catcalls come cascading down from Mile High Stadium. But in the play-offs, as usual, Elway stepped forward and took charge.

Elway had to rally the Broncos continuously in their opening-round game. And deep into the fourth quarter, they still trailed the stubborn Steelers, 23–17. But then, as if responding to a wish, Elway led Denver on a 71-yard drive for the winning touchdown as the Broncos escaped with a 24–23 win.

After the game, Dennis Smith, remembering the abuse that Elway had suffered throughout the season, walked over to his teammate and said, "I don't care what anybody says. You're the man, and you always will be the man."

Denver had dodged one bullet, but next up for the Broncos were the Cleveland Browns, making it the third time in four years that the teams had met for the AFC championship. The two previous games had produced epic encounters that have remained etched in the minds of football fans everywhere. In the first of these games, following the 1986 season, Elway drove Denver 98 yards to the tying score with only 39 clicks left on the clock. And then in overtime, he led them on a 60-yard drive that positioned the winning field goal. The next year Elway and Cleveland quarterback Bernie Kosar played "Can You Top This?" until Browns running back Ernest Byner fumbled the ball away inside Denver's five-yard line with 1:05 left in the game, as Cleveland was going in for the tying score.

But for the better part of three quarters, this year's game was as simple as a nursery rhyme. Denver took a 24–7 lead, and it looked like clear sailing. But then, as suddenly as a summer storm, Kosar led the Browns to two touchdowns in just over two minutes and cut Denver's lead to 24–21. "I was a little bit worried," admitted Elway. "After 'The Drive' and 'The Fumble,' I could see this becoming known as 'The Comeback.' "

But Elway turned the game around by leading the Broncos on an exciting 80-yard drive that broke the back of the Browns' rally and sent Denver on to a 37–21 win, and a date in New Orleans against the 49ers. Elway, who had been spectacular, drew raves from Dan Reeves. "That's the best game I've ever seen him play." And wide receiver Mark Jackson, noting that Elway had also led Denver in rushing, was all smiles. "That's what he used to do all the time —run and throw. It used to be the wild, wild west, and that's the way it was today."

"This is the best we've played," beamed a jubilant

John Elway. The big problem for the Broncos, though, was that even their best might not be nearly good enough against the heavily favored 49ers. The new and supposedly improved defense had allowed a sore-armed Kosar to sting them for 21 points, after a 9–7 Steeler squad had stretched them to their limit. And if Kosar, with a wounded wing, could put it in the air, then how high would Montana and his All-Pro playmates soar against Denver's defense? The Denver players reacted with predictable anger to that suggestion. "It's ridiculous," said cornerback Tyrone Braxton. "We're bitter that we're not getting the respect that we deserve."

The critics' views were also colored by the fact that the Broncos were 0–3 in Super Bowl appearances, including wipeouts by the Washington Redskins in Super Bowl XXII and the Giants in Super Bowl XXI. And the court of opinion wasn't completely buying the claim of Dennis Smith, and the rest of the Broncos, that "this is a better team than we've had in the past, especially defense. We're better on offense, too. We've got better players all around."

But even if the supporting cast was stronger, the main concern for Denver's opponents was still its star, Elway. As Ronnie Lott put it, "Elway can make things happen so quickly that he can induce a state of panic in a defense."

But Elway had played poorly in his two previous Super Bowl appearances. And as well as he had played in the play-offs, Montana had played even better. Montana had taken the art of quarterback play to a new level. As one NFL scout noted, "It was like a professional quarterback coming back to his high school and running a drill. I've never seen a quarterback make it look as easy as Joe does."

Going into the big game, it was obvious that the ghosts of past failures still haunted Elway. "We feel like we've let two go by already," he said, speaking about the blowout losses to Washington and New York. "And we'd hate to see a third go by. The monkey on our back seems to get bigger with each one." Meanwhile, Montana, already a three-time Super Bowl winner, was licking his lips after watching films of Denver's defensive schemes. "I can't wait," he told his offensive coordinator, Mike Holmgren.

After Denver took the opening kickoff and misfired on three straight plays, Montana's waiting was over. Artfully mixing his plays, Montana marched the 49ers 66 yards and finished off the drive with a 20-yard scoring strike to Jerry Rice, who spun away from a missed tackle by Denver safety Steve Atwater at the seven-yard line. "I tried to knock his block off, but I didn't wrap him up," said Atwater, who before the game said that he was going to pop the 49ers' receivers. But that just fired Rice's engines. "I was tired of hearing all that talk. When I came out for the game, I was all pumped up."

Halfback Bobby Humphrey then spearheaded a Denver drive that resulted in a 42-yard field goal by David Treadwell that cut the 49ers' lead to 7–3. But after the Denver defense had held the 49ers offense in check, Humphrey coughed up the ball after being hit by defensive end Kevin Fagan. Safety Chet Brooks recovered the fumble, and ten plays later Montana teamed up with tight end Brent Jones on a seven-yard toss that upped the 49ers' lead to 13–7. Mike Cofer was wide on his P.A.T. try, which turned out to be the 49ers' only miscue on an extraordinary day.

The second quarter started out as a carbon copy of the first, as Denver ran three plays and punted, and the 49ers countered with a long scoring drive that increased their lead to 20–3. Fullback Tom Rathman, who caught three passes and kept the drive alive with a fourth-down run, scored the TD on a one-yard blast up the middle.

Later, with time running out in the half, John Taylor broke off a long punt return that set the 49ers up in excellent position near midfield. And Montana and Rice cashed in the opportunity by connecting on a 38-yard scoring pass that stretched the 49ers' lead to 27–3. "You don't think it's ever going to be that easy," said Montana. "Guys couldn't wait to get back on the field."

When the second half started, the 49ers just picked up where they had left off. Linebacker Mike Walter picked off Elway's first pass of the third quarter, and one play later Rice gathered in a 28-yard scoring pass from Montana, his third of the game and a new Super Bowl record. On Denver's next possession, Elway threw another wayward pass that was picked off by Chet Brooks. Two plays later Montana froze Atwater with a pump fake to Rice and then delivered a 35-yard scoring strike to Taylor that increased the 49er lead to 41–3. Retired 49er Randy Cross, watching his former teammates score at will while Denver appeared dazed and defenseless, compared the rout to a lopsided prize fight: "There should be somebody to call off the game," he said.

When the punchless Broncos finally did manage to push across a score late in the third quarter, the 49ers answered right back with two fourth-quarter touchdowns that put the finishing touches on their 55–10 win. The 49ers' point total was the highest in Super Bowl history and their margin of victory was also the widest.

"I couldn't believe the score," said an amazed Roger Craig. "We were scoring at will and our defense played so well. It was just unreal. It was like *The Twilight Zone*"

But, according to Wade Phillips, who had seen his team join the Minnesota Vikings as the only four-time Super Bowl losers, it was more like *Mission Impossible*. "They did the same thing to the Rams and the Vikings. I thought it would be different with us, but it wasn't."

And once again, John Elway had come up short in the big game. The 49ers' defense negated his extraordinary ability, and made him seem less than ordinary. But after the game, John stood tall and didn't try to dodge the media or deny his dismal performance. And he wasn't about to become a quitter. "You bet I want to go to bat again. I'll keep going to bat every year, even if we keep losing."

The 49ers, meanwhile, had joined the Steelers as the only four-time winners of the Super Bowl and achieved their goal of repeating as champions. But before they had even allowed themselves to savor their victory in Super Bowl XXIV, Joe Montana, who had just won his third Super Bowl MVP award after completing the most amazing postseason performance in NFL history, was looking ahead to next year. "Let's go get another," he said. And before the 49ers had even peeled off their uniforms, they had set a new challenge for themselves, and coined a new word: "Three-peat."

SUPER BOWL XXV

January 27, 1991

NEW YORK GIANTS vs.
BUFFALO
"Upset"

THE NEW YORK GIANTS rode a 13–3 record to the top of the NFC East, the strongest division in the NFL. Then the Men from the Meadowlands went on to crush the Chicago Bears in a divisional playoff game before beating the San Francisco Forty-Niners in a breathtaking conference championship game.

The Giants powered their way to Tampa, the site of Super Bowl XXV, with a bedrock defense that ranked as the league's toughest and a ball-control, battering-ram-like offense that crunched out yardage in small chunks while eating up larger pieces of the clock.

The Giants were a big team, built to the specifications of head coach Bill Parcells, a believer in power football. They were a rough, resilient and resourceful squad of mostly veteran players, who played the straight-ahead, in-your-face style that Parcells taught. And they played the game with the nearly mistake-free precision that Parcells demanded.

"If they fumble, or throw interceptions, they'll be playing somewhere else," declared Parcells.

The Giants, strangely, were a team devoid of superstars. On defense, the only players selected for the Pro Bowl were linebackers Pepper Johnson and Lawrence Taylor, once the greatest player in the game, but now past his prime. Yet as a unit, they had meshed together to hold opponents to a league-low total of 211 points. Offensively, the Giants had ranked only 17th in yards gained and 13th in points scored with 335, but they had practiced Parcells' preachings by turning the ball over only 14 times in 16 games, a new NFL record.

The Giants had started the season with a 10 game winning sreak, before going into a tailspin that saw them drop three out of their next four games. During the third loss, a 17-3 beating by the Buffalo Bills, the Giants season seemed to go down the drain when their quarterback, Phil Simms, went out with a broken foot. Simms, the MVP of Super Bowl XXI and the NFC's leading passer for 1990, was replaced by Jeff Hostetler, a perennial backup who had started only two games in his seven-year NFL career as a bench-warmer with the Giants.

The Giants, though, didn't panic, adapting to Parcells' attitude that you play with the hand you were dealt, and Hostetler stepped right up and led them to two season-ending victories. Hostetler was short on experience, but he had a strong arm and his fine scrambling ability added a new dimension to the Giants attack. "He likes to run and he runs well," observed Chicago Bears head coach Mike Ditka. "He can make a big play and hurt you."

Parcells, however, wasn't expecting any playoff heroics from Hostetler. He merely wanted him to play his part and minimize his mistakes. "Hoss just has to play within his own capabilities. He's prepared himself as best he can, and he's done fine. But we're starting the playoffs now; this is *show-time*."

Hostetler showed that he was up to the challenge by leading the Giants to a 31-3 blowout of the Bears, who had won the Central Division title with an 11-5 record. "That was our best game in the last two or three years," declared fullback Maurice Carthon.

Although Hostetler didn't fill the air with footballs, he did deliver two touchdown strikes, while directing a running game that racked up 194 yards, despite the loss of its featured back, rookie Rodney Hampton, who went out with a broken foot after only two carries. Hostetler also provided a big spark with his scrambling, netting 43 yards on six scampers, including two fourth-down conversions and a 3-yard touchdown run. "He was making plays out of plays that weren't there," said wide receiver Stephen Baker, who had scored the Giants' first touchdown on a 21-yard pass from Hostetler.

Defensively, the Giants also rose to the occasion by executing a game plan that was designed to shut down a Bears ground game that had averaged more than 150 yards per contest during the season. Moving out of their traditional 3–4–4 alignment, and into a virtual 6-man front to clog the line of scrimmage, the Giants defense held the Bears to only 27 yards rushing, their lowest total in 23 years. "That's Giants football," exclaimed nose tackle Erik Howard. "They were the best pure running team in the league, but after the battle was over, we were the ones who were standing."

Despite their dominating performance against the Bears, however, the Giants' prospects were less than promising, because their road to Tampa went through San Francisco, where the 49ers were primed to become the first team to string together three consecutive Super Bowl wins.

The 49ers were a powerhouse team that had posted a league-best 14–2 record for the second successive year. They were a balanced, efficient machine whose high-scoring offense was operated by quarterback Joe Montana and included wide receiver Jerry Rice, players who were passing through the NFL on their way to the Hall of Fame. Defensively, the team was anchored by another living legend, safety Ronnie Lott, and linebacker Charles Haley, who had led the NFC in sacks.

Focusing on Montana's All-World credentials versus Hostetler's 5-game NFL resumé, the experts had made the

49ers an overwhelming choice to chop the Giants down to size. Even Bears coach Mike Ditka, who had watched the Giants demolish his team, was on the San Francisco bandwagon. "No one's going to beat the 49ers," he declared.

But the Giants weren't buying the predictions. "It really doesn't matter what's said in the paper or what the point spread is," said Carl Banks. "We have our own expectations, and we're coming to play."

The Giants' plan was to take away the big-play capabilities of the 49ers by double-covering Rice and the 49ers' other wide receiver, John Taylor, while mounting a massive pass rush against Montana. And except for a 61-yard touchdown strike to Taylor, the Giants executed their plan to perfection. "We hit Montana clean and hard, again and again," said Lawrence Taylor. And on one particular hit, late in the fourth quarter, defensive end Leonard Marshall sacked Montana and put him out of the game.

The Giants, though, were still trailing 13–9 with time running out and facing a fourth down on their own 46-yard line. But instead of giving the ball back to the 49ers, the Giants faked a punt and Gary Reasons, the blocking back on the punting team, rambled 30 yards to put the ball deep in Niners territory. A minute later Matt Bahr kicked his fourth field goal and the Giants had cut their deficit to 13–12.

"I said before the game that Coach Parcells is one guy who's going to roll the dice," said Ronnie Lott. "You have to have guts and character to pull a fake. It takes more than understanding the X's and O's to win a championship. It takes guys who are willing to take chances."

The 49ers, though, still had the lead and the ball, and they were running down the clock. But with only 2:36 left in the game, nose tackle Erik Howard jarred the ball away from Niners running back Roger Craig, and Lawrence Taylor swooped in and snatched it out of the air to give the Giants one last chance.

Hostetler, under heavy pressure, hit two big pass plays to move the ball inside the 49ers' 30-yard line with just over a minute left to play. After three running plays had moved the ball down to the 24-yard line, there were only 4 seconds left in the game. Then Matt Bahr came in to kick the game-winning field goal, and as Hostetler jumped up and shot both arms up into the air, Bahr smiled at him and said softly, "Tampa."

The Buffalo Bills captured their third consecutive AFC East title with a tops-in-the-conference 13–3 record. Then the Bills overran the Miami Dolphins and Los Angeles Raiders to earn their trip to Tampa.

The Bills saw themselves as the team of the 90's, and lots of football people agreed with that assessment. The Bills were loaded with talent on both sides of the ball, boasting nine Pro Bowl selections, including special teams player Steve Tasker. On defense they featured end Bruce Smith, who was the NFL Defensive Player of the Year, and a trio of Pro Bowl linebackers, including: Cornelius Bennett, Shane Conlan and Darryl Talley. But it was the Bills offense—the top scoring unit in the league—that made them something special.

Jim Kelly, who had finished the season as the league's top-rated passer, was the leader of a supercharged scoring machine that also featured Thurman Thomas, a gifted receiver as well as an elusive runner, who had led the league in total yards from scrimmage, and who was generally considered to be the best all-around running back in the game. The receivers included Pro-Bowler Andre Reed, veteran James Lofton, one of the leading pass catchers in NFL history, and the quick-footed, sure-handed tight end, Keith McKeller. The offensive line was led by another Pro Bowl player, center Kent Hull. "We have a lot of weapons," advised Hull, "but it all comes down to Kelly. He's the trigger man who makes it all work."

Kelly directed a quick-strike, no-huddle attack that was football's answer to the fast break. Instead of huddling after each play, the Bills went directly to the line of scrimmage where Kelly would call a play before the opposing defense could make substitutions, or even catch its breath. "It's an unbelievable offense," declared Kelly. "Give me some time to throw, and with the weapons I have, there's no stopping us."

Which is exactly what the Miami Dolphins discovered when they traveled to Rich Stadium to battle the Bills in a divisional playoff contest. The snow began falling early, but it was the Miami defense that was melted in the heat of the Bills barrage. With Kelly back at the throttle after being sidelined for four weeks with a knee injury, the Bills broke on top, 20–3. "Every throw was on the money," marveled Frank Reich, Kelly's understudy. But then a Dolphins rally, led by quarterback Dan Marino, closed the gap to 30–27 early in the fourth quarter.

Kelly quickly put a damper on the Dolphins' hopes, though, as he led the Bills on a long drive that Thurman Thomas capped with his second score of the game. And after a fumble recovery on the ensuing kickoff, Kelly and crew went in for the kill with a 26-yard strike to Andre Reed. "I thought we were going to make it real interesting when we got it down to three points, but we couldn't stay with them," acknowledged Dolphins coach Don Shula after the Bills 44–34 win.

"If the field had been dry, I could have had 300 yards today," crowed Reed, who finished with 122 yards and a pair of touchdown catches. "We're pretty scary right now," added Bruce Smith. "And we're getting better every week."

The Bills backed up Smith's boast the following week by routing the Los Angeles Raiders, 51–3, in the most lopsided result in AFC championship history. The Bills "D" did its part by holding LA to a single field goal while picking off six passes, 2 by Darryl Talley. The Bills offense, meanwhile, ripped right through the Raiders' shell-shocked defense, scoring on three of their first four possessions and piling up the points so quickly that the game was out of reach by the end of the first half. "We knew what was coming, we saw it on film all week," said Raider linebacker Riki Ellison. "But we just couldn't stop them."

The Bills' win against the Raiders put them into the Super Bowl for the first time in the history of the franchise. However, head coach Marv Levy and his team weren't interested in only making an appearance at Tampa Stadium. "There's one more river to cross," Levy reminded his players. And in case anyone didn't get the message, Bruce Smith spelled it out. "Our goal isn't to play in the Super Bowl, but to win it."

Which is what the cocky Bills and their high-flying, no-huddle offense were favored to do against the grind-it-out Giants. "This offense is limitless," declared Andre Reed. "The Raiders saw it on film, Miami saw it on film, too. We'll keep doing it until somebody stops it."

The Giants, though, weren't about to become intimidated by their underdog role or the Bills' boasting. "Let me tell you what frightens me," said Parcells. "Spiders, snakes and the IRS. The no-huddle isn't the problem. The problem is Jim Kelly, Andre Reed, James Lofton, and Thurman Thomas, the guys who work their offense. The tactic can be a little unsettling, but the no-huddle isn't going to win the game."

The Giants strategy was to control the clock with long drives that would keep the Bills offense on the sidelines for long stretches of time. And when the Bills did have the ball the Giants deployed their defense in a 2–4–5 alignment. With only two down linemen, Giants defensive coordinator Bill Belichick knew that Kelly would have time to throw, but by using four linebackers and five defensive backs Belichick was betting that the Giants could blanket the Bills receivers while containing Thurman Thomas.

The Giants two-pronged plan panned out perfectly on the first two series, as their defense twice forced the Bills to punt the ball away after running only three plays. And then Hostetler, staying mostly on the ground, led the offense on a drive that consumed over six minutes and ended with Bahr kicking a 28-yard field goal to give the Giants a 3–0 lead.

But the Bills struck back with snake-like quickness as Kelly uncoiled a 61-yard strike to Lofton that set up Scott Norwood's 23-yard field goal, knotting the score at 3–3.

The Giants strategy continued to short-circuit over their next four possessions, as their grind-it-out offense ground to a halt while Hostetler was beaten, bruised and knocked silly.

The Bills, meanwhile took a 10–3 lead early in the second quarter when Kelly led them on a 12-play, 80-yard drive that reserve running back Don Smith finished off with a 10-yard touchdown play. Kelly, with piston-like precision, completed six straight passes, good for 62 yards on a drive that was so efficient that the Bills were never even faced with a third down situation. Then the Boys from Buffalo upped their lead to 12–3 when Bruce Smith came crushing through the Giants backfield and dropped Hostetler in the end zone for a safety.

The Bills then had the chance to drop the hammer, but the Giants defense began to turn the momentum of the game back in their direction by punching out the Bills in three plays and forcing a punt. The Giants "D" rose up on the Bills on their next possession, too, as Carl Banks put a big-time hit on Andre Reed and dropped him two yards shy of the first down marker.

Given that reprieve, Hostetler took the Giants 87 yards with a quick-strike scoring drive that just barely beat the halftime whistle. Hostetler capped the drive with a 14-yard floater to Stephen Baker in the left corner of the end zone, cutting the Bills' margin to 12–10.

The Giants, picking up where they had left off, started the third quarter in championship style by traveling 75 yards in a 14-play scoring drive that ate 9:29 off the clock, the longest drive time in Super Bowl history. The Giants showed their true grit on the drive, converting four third-down tests, including a 24-yard run by O.J. Anderson and a Play-Of-The-Day catch and run by wide receiver Mark Ingram. Facing 3rd and 13 at the Buffalo 32-yard line, Hostetler, under pressure, hit Ingram with an 8-yard pass, hoping to at least get the Giants into Matt Bahr's field goal range. Ingram, though, faked out one defender, turned upfield, and broke free from Darryl Talley. As safety Mark Kelso came up to make a hit, Ingram juked around him, and before the whirling dervish was taken down by James Williams, he twisted forward just enough to stretch the ball across the first down marker. Five plays later, O.J. Anderson, who was selected as the game's MVP, bowled over left tackle for the score, that put the Giants up 17–12.

The Bills, though, bounced back in Buffalo style, going 63 yards in 4 plays, including a 31-yard touchdown burst by Thurman Thomas on the first play of the fourth quarter, that put the Bills back on top 19–17. So almost before the Bills "D" had had a chance to catch its breath, it was back on the field, trying to stop the tide of another Giant drive. This one went for 14 plays, covered 74 yards, half of which were picked up on three tosses from Hostetler to tight end Mark Bavaro, and used up another 7:32 of clock time. And when the drive stalled at the Bills 3-yard line, Bahr calmly kicked a field goal that gave the Giants a 20–19 lead. "There was no way our defense could hang in there with the Giants after so many long drives," admitted Cornelius Bennett. "You'd expect a defense to wear out, and we did."

But the Bills did not go down quietly. On their last possession of the day, Kelly drove the team relentlessly down the field, giving Scott Norwood the chance, with 4 clicks left on the scoreboard clock, to kick a 47-yard field goal and pull out the win for the Bills. But as all eyes turned toward the goal posts, Norwood's kick sailed wide right as the final whistle blew. "I thought the wind would blow it back in," said Norwood, sadly. "But it just stayed out there. It just stayed out there and wouldn't hook."

The two teams had provided football fans around the world with the most competitive Super Bowl of all time, and filled the day with extraordinary efforts and brilliant memories. "What more can you ask from a football game?" asked a jubilant Jeff Hostetler, the backup quarterback who had become a Super Bowl hero.

In the final analysis, the Giants prevailed because they controlled the clock—holding the ball for a Super-Bowl-record 40:33—and stifled the Bills' style of play. "We made them do things they didn't want to do," noted Giants cornerback Mark Collins. "I've coached a long time and I can tell you one thing," chimed in coach Parcells. "Power wins football games." And then he added, with a great big grin, "For me, it just doesn't get any better than this."

SUPER BOWL XXVI

January 26, 1992

WASHINGTON vs. BUFFALO

"Hog Heaven"

THE WASHINGTON REDSKINS won the NFC Eastern Division with an NFL-best 14–2 record and then went on to annihilate the Atlanta Falcons in a divisional playoff game and the Detroit Lions in the conference championship game on their way to a Super Bowl date at the Metrodome in Minneapolis.

Washington set the tone for their season in their opening game by destroying the Lions in their first meeting, 45–0. And they kept the beat going by reeling off 11 straight wins before their first loss, 24–21, to the Dallas Cowboys. Their only other misstep in an otherwise perfect season was a meaningless loss to the Philadelphia Eagles in the final game of the season. "We know we aren't a great team, and that we have to play hard and together to win," said head coach Joe Gibbs, "and that's what we did."

Washington was a deep and balanced team, though, which had led the NFL in scoring with 485 points, while yielding only 244.

Individually, Mark Rypien had emerged as a top-flight quarterback, finishing the season with the second best passing rating in the league. Rypien had led the NFC in passing yardage and in touchdown tosses, with 28, while throwing only 11 interceptions and earning the selection as the conference's starting quarterback in the Pro Bowl. "Rypien," declared Gibbs, "had a great year."

On the receiving end of most of Rypien's passes was an incredibly talented trio of wide receivers, known collectively as the Posse. Art Monk, the veteran of the group, had ranked fifth in the NFC during the season with 71 catches and 1049 yards while grabbing 8 touchdown passes. Monk, an ageless wonder, had finished the 12th season of his extraordinary career as the second leading pass catcher in NFL history with 801 receptions, only 18 behind the retired Steve Largent. "Art Monk is a special player," said Detroit Lionbacker Chris Spielman. "He's a Hall of Famer." Gary Clark placed right behind Monk with 70 receptions, while racking up 1,340 yards for an NFL-best 19.1-yard average and 10 touchdowns. Rickey Sanders, the third member of the Posse, was a long-ball threat and a big-game player who had piled up 193 receiving yards in Super Bowl XXII, the second highest total in Super Bowl history.

The running chores were handled primarily by Earnest Byner, a big back who had rumbled for 1,048 yards, the fourth best mark in the NFC. Rookie Ricky Ervins had added dash and 680 yards to Washington's ground game, while compiling a 4.7 yards-per-carry average. And when Washington got the ball close to the goal line, they usually rang for Gerald Riggs, who responded to the peal of the bell by bucking for 11 touchdowns. "That's my role. Come in and move the pile."

Washington's huge offensive line was nicknamed the Hogs. They were led by Pro Bowlers Jim Lachey, the best tackle in football, and guard Mark Schlerbreth. The other members of the Swine Set included tackle Joe Jacoby, guard Ralph McKenzie and center Jeff Bostic, the piglet of the line who, at only 6–2 and 278 pounds, lowered the average weight of the Hogs to 290 pounds. The Hogs were as good as they were big, blasting huge holes for the running backs while allowing only 9 sacks during the season, 10 less than the next lowest total in the league. "They're like Mack Trucks rolling over Toyotas," laughed Ervins. And Washington also had a first-rate point producer in place kicker Chip Lohmiller, who had topped the NFL in scoring with 149 points, 28 ahead of his closest competitor, Pete Stoyanovich of the Miami Dolphins.

Washington's top defenders included cornerback Darrell Green, one of the NFL's fastest runners and a perennial All-Pro pick; Wilbur Marshall, one of the best all-around linebackers in the league who, like Green, had intercepted five passes during the season; and Charles Mann, a Pro Bowl defensive end, who had recorded 11 of Washington's total of 50 sacks.

No one would have blamed the run-and-shoot Atlanta Falcons if they had felt a little gun-shy about returning to Robert F. Kennedy Stadium, where they had been shot down during the season by a 56–17 score. Rypien had riddled the Atlanta secondary for 442 yards, while equalling a club-record 6 touchdown tosses, including two long distance connections to Clark of 82 and 61 yards and another to Monk for 64 yards.

The Falcons, though, had taken flight since the debacle, winning five out of their final six regular season games to finish at 10–6, a game behind the New Orleans Saints, winners of the NFC's western division race. The Falcons continued to soar with a win over the Saints in a wild-card playoff game, but then they were forced to fly to the nation's capital, where Washington was waiting to clip their wings in a divisional playoff game. Although the Falcons managed to keep the score tighter than they had in the previous game, the result was still the same, with Washington using a total team effort to win 24–7 on a wet and muddy field. The hard-hitting Washington defense kept Atlanta bottled up all day, picking off four passes and recovering two fumbles. And Ricky Ervins meanwhile, splish-splashed for 104 yards, while Gerald Riggs popped for two short-range scoring blasts.

The NFC championship game rematched Washington against a Detroit team that had gone on to win the NFC central division with a 12–4 record before destroying Dallas 38–6 in a divisional playoff game. So even though Washington had demolished Detroit earlier in the season, they weren't about to take them, and their red-hot quarterback, Erik Kramer, lightly. "The Lions are loaded with talent at receiver and on the line," said Washington's defensive coordinator, Richie Petitbon. "And in Barry Sanders, they've got one of the greatest running backs in the game, who was injured when we played them in September. I respect their offense. It's high-tempo. It's scary."

Washington's defense, though, quickly took the roar out of the Lions by turning two turnovers into a 10–0 lead before the game was five minutes old. Constant pressure by Mann, as well as linebackers Andre Collins and Wilbur Marshall, who had 3 sacks, contained Kramer and Sanders, who was held to 44 rushing yards.

Offensively, Washington piled up the points on two touchdown bursts by Riggs, a pair of field goals by Lohmiller and a couple of air mail specials from Rypien to Clark, for 45 yards, and to Monk for 21 yards. Then Darrell Green closed out the scoring with a 32-yard interception return that made the final tally 41–10.

Washington had come a long way, but neither the players nor the coaching staff were ready to celebrate. "I want this one more than the others," said head coach Joe Gibbs, who had guided Washington to two previous Super Bowl victories. "I think, too, that some of the older guys sense this might be their last try." "As a team, we've accomplished a lot of goods things," added Rypien. "But it's not over yet."

The Buffalo Bills stampeded to their second successive 13–3 record, tops in the AFC. After nailing down their fourth consecutive Eastern Division title, the Bills had gone on to crush the Kansas City Chiefs in a divisional playoff game before beating the Denver Broncos in the conference championship game and securing a return berth to the Super Bowl.

The Bills had won with a turbo-charged offense that had led the league in yardage gained, with 6,525, while lighting up the scoreboard for 458 points, joining Washington as the only other team to score more than 400 points. Jim Kelly had had another banner season, leading the AFC with 33 touchdown passes while throwing for 3,844 yards. Pro Bowler Andre Reed was at the receiving end of 81 of those passes, accounting for over 1,000 yards gained and 10 touchdowns. James Lofton, selected to appear in his eighth Pro Bowl game, had also eclipsed the 1,000 yard mark in receptions for the season, and was now only 55 yards shy of breaking Steve Largent's all-time NFL record of 13,089 receiving yards.

Thurman Thomas, meanwhile, had solidified his standing as the best running back in the league by leading the NFL in yards from scrimmage for the third consecutive season. He had run for an AFC-best, 1,407 yards and added another 631 yards on 62 pass receptions while being named the NFL Player of the Year and the NFL's MVP. "He's just a devastating player," said teammate Jim Kelly. "I haven't seen anyone stop him yet."

Defensively, though, the Bills had had big problems, ranking 27th and next to last in the league in yards allowed. And while it was true that All-Pro end Bruce Smith and nose tackle Jeff Wright had missed big chunks of the season with injuries, other teams had also lost key players while performing much better. About the only shining lights on that dim unit were Pro Bowl linebackers Darryl Talley and, especially, Cornelius Bennett, who recorded nine of Buffalo's meager total of 31 sacks. "All year he played football like a dog chasing a cat," said Walt Corey, Buffalo's defensive coordinator.

The Bills had plenty of reason to be concerned about their divisional playoff game against the Kansas City Chiefs, a team that had blown them out, 33–6, in a Monday night game earlier in the season. The Kansas City ground game had gouged the Bills defense for 247 yards, with two backs, Christian Okoye and Harvey Williams, gaining more than 100 yards each. Barry Word had since taken over as the featured back in the Kansas City attack, and he had gone over the century mark in three straight contests, including

Kansas City's 10–6 wild-card game win over the Los Angeles Raiders.

But the Bills paid back Kansas City when it counted most, by knocking them out of the playoffs, 37–14. "They beat us like dogs," admitted Word, who was held to only 50 yards rushing. Unconcerned with Kansas City's weak passing game, the Bills had played Talley and Bennett close to the line to stuff the running game and they had responded by combining for 13 tackles. "They played us perfectly," said Word.

And while the Bills rejuvenated "D" was shutting down the Kansas City offense, Jim Kelly and Andre Reed jumpstarted the Bills offense with two long-distance scoring strikes that helped Buffalo take a 17–0 lead at halftime. "They're so tough to defend," said Jayice Pearson, the cornerback who was victimized on Reed's two scores. "They nickel and dime you until you get sucked up near the line of scrimmage, and then—bang—they hit you with a big play."

Then Kelly teamed up with James Lofton on a short touchdown toss early in the third quarter to put the game out of Kansas City's reach. Thurman Thomas played his part in the winning effort by going over the 100 yard mark, while Scott Norwood kicked in with three field goals.

In the AFC championship game, the Bills were matched up against the Denver Broncos, who had won the AFC west with a 12–4 record, and who were coming off a thrilling come-from-behind 26–24 win against the Houston Oilers in a divisional playoff game. With no timeouts remaining, John Elway, Denver's quarterback, had led the team on an 87-yard march to position David Treadwell's winning field goal with only 16 seconds left in the game. And although Denver had the AFC's best defense, it was Elway's extraordinary ability to put points on the board quickly and under pressure that caused the Bills concern. "I'm telling you, the guy is amazing," offered Bruce Smith. "He does whatever is necessary to win."

But neither Elway nor the high-octane Bills offense were factors in a 10–7 game that was totally dominated by the defenses. "Our defense is becoming a monster," raved Bills line coach Chuck Dickerson. "I was having a hard time getting the slobber off my chin, I was so excited watching them."

Cornelius Bennett, who spent almost as much time in the Denver backfield as Elway, was the biggest monster, dropping runners behind the line three times. "That's the greatest game he's ever played," declared Bills head coach, Marv Levy. Bennett's linebacking mate, Carlton Bailey, also came up big by intercepting an attempted screen pass by Elway in the third quarter and returning it 11 yards for the Bills' only touchdown. Then cornerback Kirby Jackson killed Denver's last hope when he stripped the ball away from running back Steve Sewell and then recovered the fumble he had caused. "It was our defense's day," declared Levy. "They made the plays."

It was fortunate for the Bills that their defense did rise up, because the offense disappeared. And if Denver place kicker David Treadwell hadn't hit the right upright on two makeable field goals, the Bills season might have ended right there. "Offensively, we did practically nothing," noted Levy. "I told them that we were going to have to play better than that to win the Super Bowl."

And winning the Super Bowl had been occupying the minds of the Bills team since their defeat in last year's big game. "Ever since last year's Super Bowl, we just wanted to get right back into it and start over," said Kelly. "We celebrated a little after the Denver game last week, but then everybody kind of wiped the smiles off their faces, because we had some unfinished business."

The Bills, though, seemed to be too haunted by their loss to the Giants, and maybe a little bit uncertain about their prospects against Washington. "To be as good as we are and not win, would be hard to take," said Steve Tasker, the Bills' Pro Bowl special teams leader. "Getting into the big one and losing again would be tough."

And perhaps because of those doubts, some of the Bills seemed to lose their focus, and began voicing complaints about the imagined lack of respect they felt they were receiving from the media, and from Washington. "Washington doesn't respect us," announced Bruce Smith. "We have to show them that our defense is good." And then Thurman Thomas was bent out of shape when Bills offensive coordinator Bill Marchibrodas referred to Jim Kelly as the Michael Jordan of the team. "I guess we must have two Michael Jordans; me and Jim." So while the bickering Bills seemed on the verge of a mutiny, Washington sailed into the Super Bowl as smoothly as if they were on The Good Ship Lollipop.

The game itself, though, started like a slap-stick comedy caper. First, the kickoff had to be done over because the ball was booted before the referee blew his whistle. And the laughs kept coming when Thurman Thomas missed the first two plays because he couldn't find his helmet. Then, after Washington had driven 89 yards and scored an apparent touchdown on a 2-yard pass from Rypien to Monk, the instant replay official ruled that Monk's right foot had come down on the end line. That was the first time in Super Bowl history that a touchdown was recalled by a replay. And when Washington tried to settle for a field goal, they came up empty again as the snap sailed through the fingers of holder Jeff Rutledge.

Next, the teams began a game of, "I don't want it you can have it," when, on the first play from scrimmage after the botched field goal attempt, Darrell Green tipped a Kelly pass that was then picked off by free safety Brad Edwards and returned to the Bills 12-yard line. Three plays later, though, Rypien returned the favor by throwing a pass that was intercepted by Kirby Jackson. So at the end of a hilariously sloppy quarter, the two highest scoring teams in the NFL had cavorted their way to a 0–0 score.

In the second quarter, though, Washington began to take control of the game by moving out to a 17–0 lead. Chip Lohmiller put up the first points of the game with a 34-yard field goal that was set up by a 41-yard pass play from Rypien to Ricky Sanders. On their next possession, Washington struck again, with Rypien finishing off a 51-yard drive with a 10-yard pass to Earnest Byner that increased their lead to 10–0.

Kelly tried to break the momentum that Washington was building by playing long-ball with James Lofton. But the plan backfired as Darrell Green picked off the pass at Washington's 46-yard line, setting up yet another score. A 34-yard slant-in from Rypien to Clark took the ball down to the Bills 15-yard stripe, and after Ervins had swept for 14 yards, Riggs plunged over the goal line to make the halftime score 17–0.

Now that Washington had wet its whistle, it was thirsty for more points and, once again, it was the defense that went to the well. On the first play from scrimmage after the second half kickoff, Kelly went back to pass. As Kelly faded back, linebacker Andre Collins burst up the middle on a delayed blitz, forcing Kelly to rush his pass toward tight end Keith McKeller. Kurt Gouveia, another Washington linebacker, swooped in front of McKeller, swiped the pass and ran it back 23 yards. One play and 2 yards later, Riggs had stretched the Washington lead to 24–0.

Then the Bills finally made a move, and battled their way back into the game by scoring 10 points on their next two possessions. First they picked up three points after a 77-yard drive that was keyed by a 43-yard pass from Kelly to Don Beebe. Then Thomas scored from 1 yard out to narrow Washington's lead to 24–10. "We thought we had them on the ropes," said Thomas.

But it was Washington who delivered the knockout blow on their next possession as they traveled 79 yards in 11 plays, with Rypien hitting Clark for a 30-yard touchdown pass that upped the score to 31–10. "That was the backbreaker," said Bills defensive end Leon Seals. "That broke the ice and the ship sunk."

Although the game was effectively over, the teams still had to play the fourth quarter. But all the extra 15 minutes did was let Lohmiller kick a pair of field goals, and allow Kelly to throw two meaningless touchdown passes that made the 37–24 final score look closer than it really was.

Washington had beat the Bills every which way. "They

were better and they showed it," admitted Levy. Their defense had stuffed the running game early, taking Thomas out of the picture and forcing Kelly to take to the airways, which he did a Super Bowl record 58 times. But when Kelly went back to throw, the rush was unrelenting and punishing. He was hurried 13 times, knocked down 10 times, sacked 5 times, and intercepted a Super Bowl record-tying 4 times. "Our defense did a great job," smiled Gibbs.

And the offense, after a shaky first quarter, was just as good as advertised. The Hogs opened holes for Ervins and Byner, while giving Rypien all the time he needed to connect with his receivers, primarily Clark, 7 catches for 114 yards, and Monk, 7 catches for 133 yards.

"This was truly a team effort," said Rypien, who was chosen as the Most Valuable Player. "There are a lot of guys who could have been MVP. It was something for all of us, not just me. This was just a great season that ended on a great note."

SUPER BOWL XXVII

January 31, 1993

DALLAS vs. BUFFALO
"Ride 'Em Cowboys"

THE DALLAS COWBOYS won the NFC East with a 13–3 record. Then they went on to defeat the Philadelphia Eagles in a divisional playoff game before beating the San Francisco 49ers in the NFC championship game and earning a trip to Pasadena to play the Buffalo Bills.

The Cowboys' road to the Rose Bowl, the site of Super Bowl XXVII, began to be paved in 1989 when a new owner, Jerry Jones, and a new coach, Jimmy Johnson, arrived in Dallas to revive a franchise that had fallen on hard times.

Johnson replaced Tom Landry, a coach who had guided the Cowboys to five Super Bowl appearances and 20 straight winning seasons between 1966 and 1985. During the final three years of Landry's tenure, however, the team went into a sudden tailspin, finally crashing to the ground with a 3–13 record in 1988.

The last place finish did have a silver lining, however, because it gave the Cowboys the first pick in the 1989 draft. And Johnson chose wisely, selecting Troy Aikman, a 14-karat quarterback who would help to lead the Cowboys back to greatness.

Johnson kept shuffling the Cowboys' roster during that first year, trying to find enough talented players to begin building a winning team. "Sometimes, you'd get in the huddle and be meeting your teammate for the first time," recalls linebacker Ken Norton, one of the few holdovers from those dark days in Dallas.

While that 1989 team was a 1–15 disaster zone, Johnson and Jones laid the groundwork for future success with a blockbuster trade with the Minnesota Vikings. Although the Cowboys dealt away their only Pro Bowl player, running back Herschel Walker, they received in return a combination of players and high draft choices that became the underpinnings of the current team.

Johnson continued to wheel and deal and upgrade the team. In 1990 they improved to 7–9, and in 1991 they soared to 11–5 and joined the playoffs as a wild card team. By the beginning of the 1992 season, all the pieces were in place and the Cowboys were ready to challenge for a championship.

Offensively, the Cowboys were a versatile and explosive team that had piled up 409 points, the second highest total in the league. The unit was loaded with prime-time players, including Aikman, who had developed into one of the premiere signal callers in the NFL, and Emmitt Smith, who had led the league in rushing in each of the past two seasons, while topping the NFL's touchdown makers in 1992 with 19. Smith was also a gifted receiver who had caught 59 passes. The team's top two wide receivers were All-Pro Michael Irvin, who caught 78 passes, good for 1396 yards and 7 touchdowns, and the quick-running, high-jumping Alvin Harper who averaged over 16 yards per grab on his 35 receptions. The tight end position was manned by Jay Novacek, a Pro Bowl player who had tallied 68 receptions during the season and was Aikman's chief go-to guy in clutch third down situations. The offensive line had also become an area of strength, with both guard Nate Newton and center Mark Stepnoski earning their initial selection to the Pro Bowl.

Although the mostly young defensive unit didn't have any

big-name players or Pro Bowl picks, they had a lot of big-time talent and finished the season as the NFL's top-rated defense. "We're like the Who Defense," joked cornerback Issac Holt. "Nobody knows who we are."

Charles Haley, a preseason pickup from the San Francisco 49ers, combined with two other ends, Jim Jeffcoat and Tony Tolbert, to rack up 31 sacks. And tackles Tony Casillas and Russell Maryland, along with linebackers Ken Norton and rookie Robert Jones, who combined for 228 tackles, helped to make the Dallas defense the hardest in the league to run against, holding opponents to a team-record 77.8 rushing yards per game. The Cowboys had also strengthened their secondary with the addition of rookie cornerback Kevin Smith and strong safety Thomas Everett, and the defense was as deep as it was good, allowing defensive coordinator Dave Wannstedt to substitute freely and always have fresh legs in the game.

The Cowboys' playoff opener was against the Philadelphia Eagles, and there was no love lost between these divisional rivals. "Dallas brings out our worst feelings and our best effort," noted Eagles running back Keith Byars. "There is a special joy in beating Philadelphia," countered Cowboy safety Thomas Everett.

The 11–5 Eagles, who were coming off a wild card win against the 12–4 New Orleans Saints, did a lot of pre-game trash-talking. But when it came to put-up time, the Cowboys blew the Eagles away, 34–10.

Aikman, making his first playoff start, began the rout with touchdown tosses to reserve tight end Derek Tennell and to Jay Novacek. And after Lin Elliot added a field goal to boost the Cowboys' lead at halftime to 17–3, Emmitt Smith ended the Eagles' hopes of bounding back when he capped the opening drive of the third quarter with a 23-yard explosion into the end zone. "They did a lot of talking, but by the end of the game they weren't saying much of anything," noted Ken Norton. "We let our actions on the field do our talking."

"They make the plays," agreed Eagles quarterback Randall Cunningham, who had been harassed all day by a relentless pass rush. "They rock you back on your heels and just keep coming. Dallas has a great team."

The Cowboys' road to Pasadena took them to San Francisco to play the 49ers, who had defeated Washington in a divisional playoff game, 20–13. The last time these two franchises had crossed paths in an NFC championship game was in 1982, when the 49ers had pulled out a one-point win on Joe Montana's last-minute, fourth-down touchdown pass to Dwight Clark. While The Catch had propelled the 49ers to the first of their four Super Bowl wins, it also signaled the end of the era of "America's Team." The current Cowboys, though, weren't interested in ancient history. "Hey, that wasn't *this* team," said Emmitt Smith. "That was a whole different ball club."

The 49ers, who boasted the league's best record, 14–2, and the NFL's highest-scoring offense, were playing the NFC championship game for the fourth time in five seasons. And while they had great respect for the Cowboys, they were supremely confident in their own abilities. "I think we're on the edge of doing something big," suggested Steve Young, the NFL's top-rated passer. "Whatever it takes," added Jerry Rice, the 49ers All-Pro wide receiver. "We're ready to go back to the dance."

The Cowboys and the 49ers were two evenly matched teams with rock-ribbed defenses and supercharged offenses. "It looked like we were playing the mirror images of ourselves," observed Jesse Sapolu, the 49ers center. "Those guys are quick and fast, just like us."

The Cowboys, though, were just a little bit quicker and a little bit faster—and 10 points better. "The difference was, they made the plays," said Sapolu.

There were lots of big plays on both sides of the line, including two touchdowns by Emmitt Smith, three sacks by Tony Casillas, and an interception by Ken Norton. The biggest play though, came late in the fourth quarter, right after the 49ers had closed to within 24–20 on a touchdown pass from Young to Rice. Instead of sitting on their slim lead and working the clock, the Cowboys went for the clincher. "That's been our style ever since I've been here," said Aikman. "Always go for it, always attack, no matter what the score is." So Aikman came out throwing and clicked on a 70-yard catch-and-run play with Alvin Harper that moved the ball down to the 49ers' 9-yard line. Then Aikman ended the dramatic drive with a 6-yard scoring dart to wide receiver Kelvin Martin that made the final score 30–20. "We're going to the Super Bowl," said Norton. "It used to be just a dream. Today we made it reality."

The Buffalo Bills put themselves behind the 8 ball with a season-ending loss to the Houston Oilers that cost them their fifth consecutive AFC East title. The defeat, which dropped the Bills' record to 11–5, meant that they would enter the playoffs as a wild card team and would need to win three games, including two on the road, to earn their way into their third successive Super Bowl. The headline in a Buffalo newspaper summed up the situation perfectly:

BILLS BEGIN LONGEST ROAD TODAY

And they would have to start traveling that longest road without their Pro Bowl quarterback, Jim Kelly, who had suffered strained knee ligaments in the loss to Houston. "We know our backs are to the wall," said the Bills' star running back, Thurman Thomas. And their long-shot possibilities seemed to disappear completely when those same Oilers, who had finished as the runners-up in the AFC Central Division with a 10–6 record, came to town for a wild card playoff game and ran up a 28–3 halftime score against the hometown Bills. "What a humiliating day," thought Bills head coach Marv Levy. "I thought our chances of winning the game were about the same as my chances of winning the New York State lottery."

While the shell-shocked Bills team gathered in the locker room, defensive coordinator Walt Corey delivered a tongue-lashing. "It's not like me to yell, but I didn't spare anybody. I hit them right between the eyes." Perhaps even more importantly, Corey also changed his defensive strategy, scrapping the dime package that the Bills were in and replacing the two extra defensive backs with linebackers Shane Conlan and Marcus Patton. "We needed to beef up the pass rush. If this was going to be a physical game, we had to get some physical players in there," said Corey.

While Corey was stoking the defensive unit, Gale Gilbert, the Bills' third-string signal caller, went over to Frank Reich, who was subbing at quarterback for Jim Kelly, and reminded Reich that in 1984 he had rallied the University of Maryland from a 31–0 halftime deficit to a 42–40 win over the University of Miami, the greatest comeback in college football history. "Hey, you did it before. There's no reason you can't do it again," reasoned Gilbert.

The pep talk obviously took a while to kick in, however, because Reich started the third quarter by throwing an interception that was returned 58 yards for a touchdown and stretched the Oilers lead to 35–3. And then the Bills' chances took another downward spiral when Thurman Thomas, their leading rusher and biggest scoring threat, hobbled off the field with a hip injury. So with a second-string backfield of Reich and Kenneth Davis, and a 32-point mountain to climb, the Bills' chances were hovering around zero. "My only hope was that they'd come back enough to make the score somewhat respectable," confessed Bills owner Ralph Wilson. "You never expect a team to come back from that type of deficit. Anybody who does is dreaming."

But Bills linebacker Darryl Talley wasn't about to accept the reality of the score, and instead ran up and down the sideline telling his teammates not to quit. "My old man told me that if you give up once, you'll give up again." Davis got the Bills started on their long climb back by bucking for a 1-yard score, and, after an onside kick recovery, Reich threaded a 38-yard touchdown pass to wide receiver Don Beebe that made the score 35–17. Reich next teamed up with wide receiver Andre Reed on two quick scoring strikes that cut the Bills' deficit to 35–31 at the end of the third quarter. Then Reich and Reed worked their magic a third time to boost the Bills into a 38–35 lead with only 3:00 showing on the clock. And although the Oilers kicked a field goal that sent the game into overtime, the Bills would not be denied. Three plays into the extra period, cornerback

Nate Odomes picked off a Warren Moon pass, and three plays later Steve Christie kicked the 32-yard field goal that completed the greatest comeback in NFL history. "When it happened in college, you think it's a once-in-a-lifetime experience," said Reich. "To do it twice is just unbelievable."

After a brief celebration, the Bills hit the road to Pittsburgh, where the 11–5 Steelers, winners of the AFC Central Division, were ready and waiting. But the revitalized Bills turned back the Steelers, 24–3, behind a smothering defense that stacked up seven sacks and an offense spearheaded by supersubs Reich, who threw for two touchdowns, and Davis, who rumbled through and around the Steeler defense for 104 yards.

And then the Bills were on the road again, heading to Miami to battle the 11–5 Dolphins, the team that had displaced them atop the AFC East. The red-hot Dolphins were coming off a 31–0 whitewashing of San Diego, in which Dolphin quarterback Dan Marino had torched the Chargers with three touchdown passes. But the Bills defense rose up and knocked Marino down four times; intercepted him twice; recovered three Dolphin fumbles; and held Miami to 33 yards rushing. And while the Bills offense, with a rusty Kelly back at the controls, was out of sync, Steve Christie clicked on five field goals and the Bills breezed to a 29–10 win.

The Bills had overcome a lot of adversity to join the Cowboys, Raiders, and the Patriots as the only wild-card teams to reach a Super Bowl. "We lost our quarterback before the playoffs," recapped Bills center Kent Hull. "Then we had to win two games on the road. To get to this point, the way we did, is incredibly gratifying."

The Bills, as usual, were loaded offensively, having finished second to the 49ers in yards gained. And the defense was playing at its peak, having yielded only 16 points over the last 10 quarters of playoff action. "This is the best team we've had since I've been here," summed up Bruce Smith, the sack leader of the Bills.

The Bills had also put their past bickerings behind them, and were focused in solely on the big game. "We've grown up a lot," declared Thurman Thomas. "The character on this team and the will to win is a lot greater than it has been," added Jim Kelly. The Bills appeared to have their act totally together, and they also had the apparent advantage of experience over the Cowboys, a team on which only two players had prior Super Bowl experience.

The Cowboys, though, weren't cowed by their lack of experience. "We didn't have any experience in NFC championship games," declared Emmitt Smith. "And we did all right against the 49ers."

But the Bills drew first blood in the Super Bowl as their special teams ace, Steve Tasker, blocked a Mike Saxon punt out of bounds on the Dallas 16-yard line. Four plays later, Thurman Thomas punched over right guard from 2 yards out and the Bills led 7–0.

Dallas was having trouble gaining any offensive traction on its first two possessions as Aikman worked out his Super Bowl jitters. "I really had to talk myself into relaxing," admitted Aikman.

The Bills, meanwhile, were on the prowl again, until Kelly, pressured by a safety blitz, threw into coverage and was picked off by free safety James Washington, the first of a Super Bowl–record nine turnovers by the Bills.

The Cowboys quickly cashed in on the miscue as Aikman connected with Michael Irvin for 20 yards down to the Bills 33, and three plays later found Jay Novacek over the middle for a 23-yard touchdown completion that evened the score at 7–7. "They started with a lot of two-deep coverage, taking the wideouts away," noted Aikman. "So I started finding Jay inside."

On the first play after the Dallas kickoff, Charles Haley drilled Kelly at the 2-yard line, forcing a pop-fly fumble that defensive tackle Jimmie Jones plucked out of the air and carried into the end zone for Dallas' second score. The touchdowns, coming only 15 seconds apart, were the quickest pair of scores in Super Bowl history.

The Bills, though, shook off their two miscues, as Andre Reed hauled in a 40-yard completion on the first play of the second quarter, down to the Dallas 4-yard line. But the Bills couldn't dent the Dallas goal line on three rushing attempts, and on fourth down Thomas Everett picked off another Kelly pass.

On the Bills' next possession, Kelly was put out of the game when Norton, coming on a blitz, was sent flying by a Bills blocker and landed on Kelly's bad knee. Playoff hero Frank Reich came off the bench and picked up where he had left off by connecting on his first two passes, including a 38-yarder to Reed down to the Dallas 22 yard line. But after Charles Haley and Russell Maryland stuffed Thomas on a third-and-one at the 3 yard line, Reich and the Bills had to settle for a field goal that cut the Cowboys lead to 14–10 with 3:24 left in the second quarter.

The Cowboys defense had come up big on two successive goal line stands, and now it was time for Aikman to air it out. With only a few minutes left in the first half, the Cowboys went into their hurry-up offense, and five plays later Aikman followed up a 38-yard gallop by Smith with a 19-yard touchdown strike to Michael Irvin. And 18 seconds later it was déjà vu time, as the Cowboys recovered a Thurman Thomas fumble, and Aikman found Irvin in the left corner of the end zone to boost the Cowboys' halftime lead to 28–10.

Despite five first half turnovers the Bills were only down by two touchdowns, 31–17, going into the fourth quarter after a Dallas field goal and a 40-yard touchdown pass from Reich to wide receiver Don Beebe on the final play of the third quarter. And after the mountain that Reich and the Bills had climbed in their comeback against the Oilers, 14 points looked like only a mole hill.

But Buffalo's hopes were quickly buried under an avalanche of their own errors and Dallas' excellence. The landslide started on the Cowboys' second possession of the quarter when Aikman fired a 45-yard scoring strike to Alvin Harper that upped Dallas' lead to 38–17. And the slide picked up speed when, less than two minutes later, Emmitt Smith zipped into the end zone on a 10-yard draw play three plays after Thomas Everett had intercepted a Reich pass. And as soon as the Bills got the ball back they gave it away again, as Reich, operating out of the shotgun formation, fumbled a high snap from center, which was scooped up by Norton and run back for a touchdown that made the final score 52–17, and made the Bills the first team to lose three consecutive Super Bowls.

The Cowboys' win, the ninth straight by an NFC team, was absolutely complete and decisive as the stars from Texas shined big and bright. Michael Irvin, for one, hauled in six receptions for 114 yards and two touchdowns, while Emmitt Smith rushed for 108 yards, caught six passes, and was a key blocker when the Bills blitzed. And Troy Aikman, who was named the game's MVP, was near-perfect, completing 22 of 30 passes for 273 yards, four touchdowns, and zero interceptions. "Offensively and defensively, Dallas just smothered them," noted Eagles coach Rich Kotite. "Dallas played the whole game as if the score was nothing-nothing. They just never let up."

SUPER BOWL XXVIII

January 30, 1994

DALLAS vs. BUFFALO

"Let's Do It Again"

THE DALLAS COWBOYS repeated as NFC Eastern Division champions with a 12–4 mark, which tied them with the Buffalo Bills and the Houston Oilers for the best record in the NFL. The Cowboys then went on to devour the Green Bay Packers in a divisional playoff game and sandbag the San Francisco 49ers to earn their second straight trip to the Super Bowl.

After the Cowboys, with the youngest team in the NFL, had gone 13–3 in 1992 and then blown away three playoff foes on their way to a record-setting win in Super Bowl XVII, it seemed as though they might not lose another game for a long time to come. But a back injury to Pro Bowl quarterback Troy Aikman, which sidelined him for most of the 1993 preseason, and a two-game holdout by star running back Emmitt Smith caused the Cowboys to stumble to an 0–2 record, including a 13–10 loss to Buffalo in Dallas.

After that loss to the Bills, linebacker Charles Haley was so incensed at the team's low morale and lack of offensive firepower that he slammed his helmet through a locker room wall. "We'll never win with a bleeping rookie running back," screamed Haley, in reference to Smith's backup, Derrick Lassic.

The Cowboys' owner, Jerry Jones, suddenly realized that without Smith the Dallas dynasty-in-the-making was about to disappear like the dinosaurs, so he quickly agreed to contract terms that made Smith the highest-paid running back in the history of the NFL.

As soon as Smith reported to practice he walked over to Michael Irvin, the Cowboys' All-Pro wide receiver and said, "Now we can get started. Let's go 14–2, get back in the Super Bowl, and win it all."

With Smith back in the lineup and Aikman back at full strength, the Cowboys actually did seem to be invincible as they reeled off seven straight victories. The streak started with a win over Phoenix that prompted the Cardinals' defensive coordinator, Fritz Shurmur, to rave, "Aikman was magnificent. It was the best I've ever seen a quarterback throw a ball. Every receiver he hit was on the run and the ball was right there." Along the way the Cowboys also stopped the 49ers, 26–17, and the Philadelphia Eagles, 23–10, in a game in which Smith sloshed through the mud at Veterans Stadium for 237 yards, the sixth best rushing performance in NFL history.

The Dallas winning string was finally snapped by the Atlanta Falcons, but it took a game in which Aikman was sidelined by an ankle injury and Smith had to hobble off the field with a bruised muscle after only one carry. The Cowboys also lost their next game, 16–14, when defensive tackle Leon Lett committed a mental miscue on a missed field goal attempt, allowing the Miami Dolphins' Pete Stoyanovich a second chance to kick the last-second game-winning three-pointer.

The Cowboys bounced back from those two losses to close out their regular season schedule with a five-game unbeaten streak, including a dramatic 16–13 overtime road win in the season finale against the New York Giants. That game allowed the Cowboys to edge out the New Yorkers in the NFC East, and to gain home field advantage throughout the playoffs. Aikman was, as usual, impeccable in the Giants game, completing 24 of 30 passes with zero interceptions. But the star of the day was Emmitt Smith who, despite suffering a shoulder separation late in the first half, continued playing and pounded out 168 yards on the ground, which was enough yardage to earn him his third consecutive rushing title. Smith also snared 10 receptions for an additional 61 yards and the Cowboys' only touchdown of the game. "Emmitt Smith is a great football player," said Dallas coach Jimmy Johnson, "and he has as much pride as any football player I've ever been around."

The Cowboys' win earned them a bye in the first round of the NFC playoffs, and while they sat and watched, the 9–7 Green Bay Pakcers upset the 10–6 Detroit Lions, who had won the NFC Central Division title, 28–24; and the 11–5 Giants mastered the 9–7 Vikings, 17–10.

The Cowboys swung into action the following week against the Packers, a team they had trounced 36–14 in the fourth game of the regular season. "But I believe we're a better team than the last time we played them," said Green Bay coach Mike Holmgren, who sounded as though he was trying to convince himself that Green Bay actually belonged on the same field with the Cowboys.

Jimmy Johnson certainly wasn't losing any sleep over the prospect of playing the Packers, despite the presence of Green Bay wide receiver Sterling Sharpe, who had broken his all-time NFL single-season reception record with 112 catches, and red-hot quarterback Brett Favre, who had teamed up with Sharpe for three TD tosses against the Lions, including the 40-yard game-winner when there were only 55 clicks left on the clock. "I can't get caught up in who we play, whether it be the Giants, or the Packers, or the Eagles, or whoever. The only thing I concern myself with is my football team. I may be somewhat biased, but I think we've got the best team going."

The Cowboys' offense, though, wasn't even good in the early going against Green Bay. During the first 17 minutes of play the usually sure-handed Cowboys turned the ball over on a fumble and a rare interception by Aikman, who had been picked off only six times during the season. The

Cowboys were also stopped on a fake punt attempt deep in their own territory when veteran Bill Bates misread the Packers' defensive alignment. Fortunately for Dallas their defense handcuffed the Packers' offense and limited the damage caused by the three miscues to one measly field goal.

The slumbering Cowboys' offense finally awoke for one sepctacular 18 minute stretch over the second and third quarters during which they struck for 24 unanswered points, paving their way to a 27–17 win over the outmanned Packers. Aikman, who passed for 302 yards and set a Dallas postseason single-game record for pass completion percentage, was the main man in the Cowboys' offensive outburst with a trio of TD tosses; he threw one each to tight end Jay Novacek and wide receivers Alvin Harper and Michael Irvin, who caught nine passes for 126 yards.

The Cowboys had played just well enough to beat a team that didn't come close to matching their talent level, but except for that 18 minutes of offensive explosiveness, they didn't gain any points for artistry or intensity. "They're the best team in the NFL, but they didn't really kill us," said Brett Favre, who sounded surprised at the relative closeness of the score.

The Cowboys, though, knew that they couldn't sleepwalk their way past the 49ers in what would be the first NFC Championship Game rematch since 1971 when, coincidentally, the Cowboys defeated the Niners for the second-straight season.

The Cowboys had watched the 49ers decimate the Giants 44–3 in the other divisional playoff contest, and they knew that they were going to have to get their game in gear if they expected to defeat the 49ers and earn the opportunity to defend their Super Bowl title. "We all know we're going to have to have to play a lot better against the 49ers," said Dallas defensive end Jim Jeffcoat, who was very well aware of the fact that the Niners had topped the NFL in scoring with 473 points, 97 more than the runner-up Cowboys. "Their offense is like the run-and-shoot. When they get going, they're going to keep it up and they can slaughter you."

The 49ers' win over the Giants was keyed by Pro Bowl quarterback Steve Young, who had finished as the league's top-rated QB for the third consecutive season, and running back Ricky Watters, who had racked up 118 yards rushing and scored an NFL postseason-record five touchdowns against a defense that had allowed the fewest points in the league during the regular season. And the much maligned 49ers defense had risen up and shut down the Giants run-oriented offense, which had produced the most productive ground game in the league during the 1993 season.

"This is the best I've ever seen a team play against us," said Bart Oates, the Giants' Pro Bowl center, as he sat in the Candlestick Park locker room. "It looked like they were on fast ponies and we were on mules," added Giants coach Dan Reeves.

Although Dallas had had to go into OT to beat that same Giants team only two weeks earlier, Jimmy Johnson was supremely confident that this team would rise to the challenge against the 49ers. "We weren't as sharp as we could have been, but I'm not concerned," said Johnson after the Cowboys' win over the Packers. "This felt like a regular-season game. The 49ers will be like a regular-season game. When you've been where we've been there's only one game that's significant," said Johnson as he stared right past the 49ers to the Georgia Dome in Atlanta, the site of Super Bowl XXVIII. Johnson was so convinced that the Cowboys would nail the Niners that he called a Dallas radio sports talk show and publicly "guaranteed" a win for the home team.

Then the Cowboys went out and made Johnson look like a prophet by rolling to a 28–7 halftime lead on their way to a 38–21 victory over the 49ers. It was simply a case of an irresistible force overcoming a very movable object as Aikman once again put on a quarterback clinic while the Dallas "D" put a vise on the 49ers high-scoring offense until the game was in the bag.

The Cowboys jumped out to a first quarter lead when

Emmitt Smith, who ran for 88 yards, slashed into the end zone from five yards out. After the Niners tied the score on a short pass from Young to fullback Tom Rathman, the Cowboys opened the corral and romped to 21 second-quarter points. Dallas fullback Daryl Johnston started the scoring spree with a four-yard bolt into the end zone that gave the Cowboys a 14–7 lead. Then the Dallas defense got the ball back into Aikman's hands when safety Thomas Everett picked off a Young pass and returned it 14 yards to the Niners' 24-yard stripe. Four plays later, Aikman made the visitors pay the price when he caught the Niners' defense double-teaming Novacek and found Smith all alone for an 11-yard TD pass. "They doubled up on Jay and totally forgot about me. I like it like that," said Smith, who caught seven passes for a game-high 85 yards.

On the Cowboys' next possession, Aikman led them on an eight-play, 72-yard drive which he capped with a 19-yard scoring strike to Novacek, who grabbed the ball and then bowled over Tim McDonald, the 49ers' All-Pro safety, and linebacker John Johnson to gain entry into the end zone and to give Dallas their 28–7 halftime lead.

The Cowboys' first-half offensive fireworks display had been perfectly complemented by a dynamic defensive effort that limited Young to 77 yards passing and completely shut down Ricky Watters only a week after he had looked like a Hall of Fame runner against the Giants. "I don't think anybody in a million years thought it would be this type of ball game," said George Seifert, the shocked head coach of the 49ers. "I felt our football team was well prepared. We just met up with a great football team that played a great game in all phases."

The 49ers looked as though they might be able to get back into the contest when Aikman was forced out of the game with a concussion on the Cowboys' first series of the third quarter. Aikman was knocked so senseless that when the Dallas team doctor asked the quarterback where the upcoming Super Bowl was going to be played he replied "Henryetta," the small Oklahoma town where Aikman had grown up.

And while the Cowboys' offense stalled under the direction of the rusty veteran Bernie Kosar, the Niners took temporary advantage of the opportunity when Watters capped a short drive with a 4-yard burst that narrowed their deficit to 28–14. Kosar, though, stifled the 49ers' momentum on the Cowboys' next possession by leading his team on an 82-yard scoring drive that he capped with a 42-yard pass-and-run TD toss to Alvin Harper that stretched the Dallas lead to 35–14 and effectively put the game out of reach. Kosar kept the drive alive by completing a critical 12-yard pass to Irvin on a third down and nine play from Dallas' 19-yard stripe. "Considering the timing, it was as big a play as there was in the game," pointed out Jimmy Johnson.

A fourth quarter field goal by Dallas kicker Eddie Murray and a too little, too late 1-yard sneak by Young closed out the scoring in a game that Dallas simply dominated. "I would never have believed that we would come down here and get beat like this. I just wouldn't have believed it," said an obviously dejected Steve Young.

"I think our players responded to the situation," said Jimmy Johnson, whose pre-game confidence proved to be completely justified. "We took charge from the opening kickoff and never let up. I wanted our team to respond to the challenge with an underlying attitude that we were not going to have any excuses. The bottom line was to win and go back to the Super Bowl."

The Buffalo Bills, with a 12–4 record, won the AFC Eastern Division title for the fifth time in six seasons. Then the Bills went on to defeat the Los Angeles Raiders in a divisional playoff game and the Kansas City Chiefs in the AFC Championship Game to earn an unprecedented fourth consecutive trip to the Super Bowl.

The Bills won their division behind an offense that finished fourth best in the AFC, but despite a defense that ranked 27th and next-to-last in the NFL. The poor showing of the Bills' defense was surprising, since they had a line that was anchored by All-Pro defensive end Bruce Smith, a linebacking corps that featured Pro Bowl performers in

Cornelius Bennett and Darryl Talley, and a defensive back-field that included cornerback Nate Odomes, who had tied for the league lead with nine interceptions.

Offensively, the Bills relied most heavily on Thurman Thomas, an all-purpose running back who had led the AFC in rushing with 1,315 yards and who had also caught 48 passes for an additional 387 yards. "There has never been a game plan we've put in that Thurman hasn't been a big part of," said Tom Bresnahan, the Bills' offensive coordinator. "In fact, he's the center of our game plan."

Jim Kelly, the Bills' perennial Pro Bowl signal caller had only had a mediocre season, a conclusion that was reflected in his 79.9 QB rating and the fact that his 18 TD tosses were matched by his 18 interceptions. Kelly, though, had thrown for over 3,000 yards, with his main target being tight end Pete Metzelaars, who had led the Bills with 68 receptions, eclipsing his total for the previous four seasons. The wide receivers included Andre Reed, Don Beebe, and newcom-ber Bill Brooks, who snared 60 passes.

The Bills' record bought them a bye in the opening round of the playoffs, which saw the 11–5 Kansas City Chiefs edge out the 9–7 Pittsburgh Steelers in a 27–24 overtime nail-biter, and the 10–6 Los Angeles Raiders romp over the 9–7 Denver Broncos, 42–24.

The Bills swung into action the following week when they hosted the red-hot Raiders in front of 62,000 fanatical fans. The temperature at game time was zero degrees Fahr-enheit, but the icy currents sweeping across Rich Stadium caused the wind chill factor to register 32 degrees below zero, creating the coldest game conditions in Buffalo's his-tory. And the Bills played the first half as though they were frostbitten, falling behind the Raiders 17–6. Kelly, though, stoked the Bills' fire in the second half by connecting on a pair of TD passes to Bill Brooks, including a 22-yard fourth quarter strike that hoisted Buffalo to a hard-fought 29–23 victory. "We took one step today, and we'll take another step next week," said Cornelius Bennett. "Then we'll go for the final step in Atlanta."

The Bills' next step was the AFC Championship Game

against the Kansas City Chiefs, who were quarterbacked by Joe Montana, considered by most football watchers to be the greatest quarterback to ever play the game. In his prime, Montana had led the 49ers to four Super Bowl championships, but injuries had idled him for all but one half of one game over the 1991 and 1992 seasons. The 49ers had traded him to the Chiefs prior to the start of the 1993 season. Montana showed that he still had some magic left in his 37-year-old arm by leading the Chiefs to their first divisional title in 22 years. Then the Living Legend rallied the Chiefs from a 17–7 halftime deficit to an overtime win in their opening round playoff game against the Steelers. "It's very simple," said Carl Peterson, the Chiefs' general manager. "He is absolutely, unequivocally the best at what he does."

The following week, Montana waved his wand again and rallied the Chiefs to a 21-point fourth quarter and a 28–20 win over the Central Division champion Houston Oilers, who had closed out the season with 11 straight wins. "We had a chance to put them away early, but we let them stay around," lamented Chris Dishman, the Oilers' All-Pro cornerback. "I said all week that we couldn't give Montana the ball in the fourth quarter with the game on the line. Look what he did. I haven't seen any quarterback throw a pass like he does."

When there were only four teams left in the Super Bowl picture, football fans seemed to fall in love with the idea of Montana squaring off against Steve Young, who had replaced him as quarterback on the 49ers, or against Aikman and the Cowboys, who had replaced the Niners as the NFL's glamour team.

But the Bills' fired up defense never allowed Montana to find his rhythm or to become a factor in the first half of the game. And early in the third quarter Montana was sent to the sidelines with a concussion when his head struck the ground after he was decked by a trio of Buffalo defenders.

The star of the Bills' 30–13 win turned out to be Thurman Thomas, who scored three touchdowns and rushed for 186 yards, the second highest total ever amassed in an AFC

Championship Game. "We just couldn't handle Thurman Thomas," summed up KC coach Marty Schottenheimer.

Thomas and Kelly, who called a nearly flawless game, were both quick to praise the work of the Bills' offensive line. "The difference was those five guys," said Kelly. "They were opening holes like you wouldn't believe. If you give us the chance, we're going to score."

The Bills never seemed to have any problems in piling up the points in AFC Championship Games, having outscored their opponents by a combined score of 120–33 in the past four title games. But the Bills' performances in their three Super Bowl appearances were an entirely different story. After a heartbreakingly close loss to the Giants in Super Bowl XXV, the Bills had been blown out by Washington and Dallas on the following two Super Sundays. So there weren't a whole lot of football fans outside of Buffalo who were very happy to see the Bills heading for Atlanta to meet the Cowboys in the first-ever back-to-back Super Bowl rematch. One witty Bills fan caught the mood of the country perfectly when he held up a sign near the end of Buffalo's win over the Chiefs that read:

"WE'RE BACK. DEAL WITH IT, AMERICA."

The Bills, too, were coming into the game with a chip on their collective shoulder as big as a boulder and a monkey on their back as large as King Kong, knowing that they could become the first team in American professional sports history to lose four consecutive championship games. "If people don't want to watch, they don't have to turn on their TVs," growled Bruce Smith.

Bills coach Marv Levy put their plight in perspective. "We've been a very good team for a long time. We've won more games in the 1990s than any other team. Probably for us to be considered a great team though, we'll have to win a Super Bowl. I think that's fair."

Although the Bills might need a Super Bowl ring to confirm their place among the elite teams in NFL history, Troy Aikman, for one, took exception to all the ridicule that had been heaped upon a team that had achieved so much. "It's a shame that people can't recognize what they've accomplished. We all realize how difficult it was for the Cowboys this year and what we had to deal with to try to make a return trip. Now, they've done it four years running. They've continued to battle this thing for four seasons. It speaks volumes for the type of people that are on their team."

The Bills' partisans were pinning their hopes on strong performances from their two offensive sparkplugs, Kelly and Thomas. Although Kelly had played well and Thomas had put on an MVP-type show against the Giants in Super Bowl XXV, the pair of them had played poorly against Washington and Dallas. Both players, though, were coming into the game in Atlanta on a roll. Thomas had rocked the Chiefs for 208 yards of total offense and Kelly had been in top form in Buffalo's two postseason victories. "He was un-believable against the Raiders," said Kent Hull, the Bills' Pro Bowl center. "That was the best game he's played in the eight years that I've been here, and he was just as sharp against the Chiefs."

"We feel good about ourselves," explained Kelly. "We're not cocky, but we have a lot of confidence in our abilities."

When it came to confidence, though, nobody could keep up with the Cowboys, the only team in the NFL to finish among the top 11 in all six major categories on both offense and defense. The Cowboys' belief in their abilities just flowed out of them like lava out of a volcano. "The Cowboys are the team of the 1990s. We're a dynasty," declared Alvin Harper. "The only team that can stop us is ourselves," added offensive tackle Erik Williams.

Before the game began, though, a controversy arose over the Georgia state flag, which includes the stars and bars of the Confederate flag, and is therefore considered offensive by many people. The NFL's commissioner, Paul Tagliabue, tried to sidestep the issue by claiming, "We are not a politi-cal advocacy group. We are a football league." But other people, including Georgia Congressman Don Lewis, thought that the NFL should have taken a more forceful stance. "This flag represents a past era in American history —a dark, evil and sad period," said Lewis. "The flag is a symbol of racism, bigotry and intolerance. The flag contradicts the ideals of sportsmanship and unity that are associated with the Super Bowl. It is an affront to the idea of fair play, goodwill, and brotherhood. The flag should not be a part of the future of Georgia." A compromise of sorts was achieved when the flag was not flown inside the Georgia Dome, but was unfurled on a pole in front of the stadium.

Once the game began it looked as though it was going to quickly turn into another blowout. Cowboys rookie Kevin Williams took the game's opening kickoff and, following a wall of white shirts, raced 50 yards to the Bills' 48-yard line. Then on the first play from scrimmage, Aikman rifled a 20-yard strike to Michael Irvin and it looked like, "here we go again." But the Bills defense dug in their heels and caused the Cowboys to settle for Eddie Murray's 41-yard field goal which, coming at the 2:19 mark, was the third quickest score in Super Bowl history.

The Bills' offense, buoyed by the determined stand of their defensive unit, bounced right back, as Kelly engineered a 43-yard drive that set up Steve Christie's Super Bowl–record 54-yard field goal. On the Bills' next possession, though, Thurman Thomas committed the first of his two costly turnovers when, after a 7-yard pickup, he was jarred loose from the ball by Dallas safety James Washington. Three plays after Darren Woodson covered the ball on the mid-field stripe, Aikman completed a 24-yard pass to Harper to the Bills' 15-yard line. But the Bills' "D" then put up another stonewall, stopping Smith on a third-and-five from their own 10-yard line, and forcing the Cowboys to settle for another Murray field goal and a 6–3 lead.

After the ensuing kickoff, the Bills picked up one first down before they were forced to punt. But when Dallas defender Dave Thomas was flagged for running into Buffalo punter Chris Mohr, the Bills were back in business on their own 46-yard line. Given a new set of downs, Kelly led the Bills on a dazzling 17-play drive that Thurman Thomas capped with a 4-yard scoring burst that gave the Bills a 10–6 lead early in the second quarter.

After an exchange of punts, the Cowboys found themselves pinned back in the shadow of their own goal line when Steve Tasker, the Bills' All-Pro special teams player, downed a Chris Mohr punt at the Dallas 1-yard line. Aikman, however, passing with pinpoint accuracy, quickly led the Cowboys into Bills' territory by completing six of seven pass attempts. But on a first down from the Buffalo 37-yard line, Aikman, under the pressure of a big pass rush from Bruce Smith, had a pass intended for Harper picked off by Odomes at the Bills' 12-yard line and returned all the way to the Dallas 47-yard line.

With 1:03 left in the half, Kelly took advantage of the turnover by passing the Bills down to the Dallas 9-yard line, and setting up Christie for a 28-yard field goal which gave the Bills a 13–6 lead to take into the locker room. "We were playing the game the way we had laid it out," said Kelly. "Take what they give you, and don't get greedy. That's exactly what we did."

Despite the fact that only six teams had ever rallied to win a Super Bowl after trailing at halftime, everyone on the Dallas team kept their cool. "Nobody panicked," said Aikman. "Everybody was very calm. Jimmy Johnson didn't say very much. We had had difficulty establishing any rhythm. Buffalo did a good job of mixing its coverage, and we kind of got away from our running game. But we knew that once we got our running game going we'd be fine."

It was Buffalo, though, who took the second half kickoff and began moving the football. But on their third play from scrimmage, the thin thread of the Bills' hold on the game started to unravel when Leon Lett stripped the ball out of the hand of Thurman Thomas. James Washington swooped down, scooped the ball up and zig-zagged his way to a 46-yard trip into the Buffalo end zone that tied the score at 13–13. "Leon stripped the ball and I just picked it up. I don't have great speed, but I wanted to get into the end zone so bad," said Washington.

"If I don't fumble it's a different ball game. I really did change the momentum," said Thomas, who spent a lot of the second half on the bench suffering from leg cramps and his third consecutive "Day of Disaster" in Super Bowl games.

The Dallas defense, feeding off the rush of Washington's TD, held the Bills to three plays—including a third down sack of Kelly—and a punt. And then the game turned into the Emmitt Smith Show. With the ball on the Dallas 36-yard line following Mohr's punt, Smith ran the ball seven times on an eight-play drive, gaining all but three of the 64 yards, and topping off his extraordinary effort with an explosive 15-yard touchdown burst on which he bounced off of would-be tacklers as though he were a pinball. "I was very possessed on that drive," said Smith. "The line starts pushing them back, we start moving the ball, and everything gets exciting. And once we scored the touchdown, I was full of joy."

"The line really picked it up on that drive, and Emmitt did what he always does," said Dallas guard Nate Newton. "He smells a hole like a bloodhound on a scent."

The teams treaded water for the remainder of the third quarter, but on the first play of the fourth quarter Kelly, with a third-and-six at the Bills 35-yard line, tried to thread a needle to wide receiver Don Beebe. The ever-present James Washington stepped in front of Beebe, picked off the pass, and returned it 12 yards to the Bills' 34-yard line. "They kept running the same pattern on third-and-5 or 6, so I thought I could make the play," said Washington.

Then Aikman went to work, leading the Cowboys on a nine-play drive that featured a 22-yard third down pass to Harper, and was capped by a 1-yard fourth down TD run by Smith that upped the Cowboys lead to 27–13. After the Cowboys defense forced another Mohr punt, Aikman and company went to work again. After three short runs by Smith and a short pass to Novacek, Aikman teamed up with Harper on a pass down to the Bills 1-yard line. And while the Cowboys were unable to punch across another touchdown, they did come away with a 30–13 lead on Eddie Murray's third field goal of the day, with only 2:50 left on the clock for Buffalo.

Kelly came out throwing and quickly, desperately moved

the Bills deep into Cowboys' territory. But on fourth and seventeen from the Dallas 22, Kelly was only able to complete a 9-yard pass to Beebe. Once again, Buffalo had come up short on Super Sunday.

Although the Bills had fulfilled everybody's worse fears and suffered another crushing defeat, they remained proud and defiant despite the fact that they had joined the Minnesota Vikings and Denver Broncos as the only franchises to drop four Super Bowls. "Anybody who calls us losers doesn't know what they're talking about," said Kelly. "We haven't won the Super Bowl, but second place is a lot better than last place. We'll keep fighting until we get it right."

The Cowboys, who had become only the fourth franchise to win consecutive Super Bowls, were already looking ahead toward an unprecedented third title as they whooped it up in their locker room. "You can't ever be satisfied," said Emmitt Smith, who had rushed for 132 yards, scored a pair of touchdowns and was named the game's MVP in a close vote over James Washington, a player who had started only one other game during the 1993 season. "There's always room for me and the team to grow," added Smith, who joined Larry Czonka, a former fullback of the Miami Dolphins, as the only player to rush for more than 100 yards in back-to-back Super Bowls.

The Cowboys' victory was the 10th consecutive Super Bowl win for the NFC. Their attitude was perhaps summed up best by guard Kevin Gogan: "Last year's game was over so fast. It was done by halftime. But this was a tight battle. This was a challenge, and we responded. It showed we're a powerhouse. It showed that you might stop us early, but you won't ever stop us in the end."

SUPER BOWL RESULTS

	WINNER	LOSER	SCORE
I	Green Bay	Kansas City	35–10
II	Green Bay	Oakland	33–14
III	NY Jets	Baltimore	16–7
IV	Kansas City	Minnesota	23–7
V	Baltimore	Dallas	16–13
VI	Dallas	Miami	24–3
VII	Miami	Washington	14–7
VIII	Miami	Minnesota	24–7
IX	Pittsburgh	Minnesota	16–6
X	Pittsburgh	Dallas	21–17
XI	Oakland	Minnesota	32–14
XII	Dallas	Denver	27–10
XIII	Pittsburgh	Dallas	35–31
XIV	Pittsburgh	LA Rams	31–19
XV	Oakland	Philadelphia	27–10
XVI	San Francisco	Cincinnati	26–21
XVII	Washington	Miami	27–17
XVIII	LA Raiders	Washington	38–9
XIX	San Francisco	Miami	38–16
XX	Chicago	New England	46–10
XXI	NY Giants	Denver	39–20
XXII	Washington	Denver	42–10
XXIII	San Francisco	Cincinnati	20–16
XXIV	San Francisco	Denver	55–10
XXV	NY Giants	Buffalo	20–19
XXVI	Washington	Buffalo	37–24
XXVII	Dallas	Buffalo	52–17
XXVIII	Dallas	Buffalo	30–13

MVP WINNERS

	Player, position	Team
I	Bart Starr QB	Packers
II	Bart Starr QB	Packers
III	Joe Namath QB	Jets
IV	Len Dawson QB	Chiefs
V	Chuck Howley LB	Cowboys
VI	Roger Staubach QB	Cowboys
VII	Jake Scott S	Dolphins
VIII	Larry Czonka RB	Dolphins
IX	Franco Harris RB	Steelers
X	Lynn Swann WR	Steelers
XI	Fred Biletnikoff WR	Raiders
XII	Tie: Randy White DT	Cowboys
	Tie: Harvey Martin DE	Cowboys
XIII	Terry Bradshaw QB	Steelers
XIV	Terry Bradshaw QB	Steelers
XV	Jim Plunkett QB	Raiders
XVI	Joe Montana QB	49ers
XVII	John Riggins RB	Redskins
XVIII	Marcus Allen RB	Raiders
XIX	Joe Montana QB	49ers
XX	Richard Dent DE	Bears
XXI	Phil Simms QB	Giants
XXII	Doug Williams QB	Redskins
XXIII	Jerry Rice WR	49ers
XXIV	Joe Montana QB	49ers
XXV	Ottis Anderson RB	Giants
XXVI	Mark Rypien QB	Redskins
XXVII	Troy Aikman QB	Cowboys
XXVIII	Emmitt Smith RB	Cowboys

If you enjoyed this book you might want to order some of our other exciting titles:

BASKETBALL SUPERSTARS ALBUM 1995, by Richard J. Brenner. Includes 16 full-color pages, and mini-bios of the game's top superstars, plus career and all-time stats. 48 pages ($4.50/$5.50 Can.)

SHAQUILLE O'NEAL*LARRY JOHNSON, by Richard J. Brenner. A dual biography of the two brightest young stars in basketball. 96 pages, 10 pages of photos. ($3.50/$4.50 Can.)

MICHAEL JORDAN*MAGIC JOHNSON, by Richard J. Brenner. A dual biography of two of the greatest superstars of all time. 128 pages, 15 dynamite photos. ($3.50/$4.25 Can.)

TROY AIKMAN*STEVE YOUNG, by Richard J. Brenner. A dual biography of the top two quarterbacks in the NFL. 96 pages, 10 pages of photos. ($3.50/$4.50 Can.)

BARRY BONDS*ROBERTO ALOMAR, by Bob Woods. A dual biography of two of the brightest stars in baseball. 96 pages, 10 pages of photos. ($3.50/$4.50 Can.)

MARIO LEMIEUX, by Richard J. Brenner. An exciting biography of one of hockey's all-time greats. 96 pages, 10 pages of photos. ($3.50/$4.50 Can.)

THE WORLD SERIES, THE GREAT CONTESTS, by Richard J. Brenner. The special excitement of the Fall Classic is brought to life through seven of the most thrilling Series ever played, including 1993. 176 pages, including 16 action-packed photos. ($3.50/$4.50 Can.)

THE COMPLETE SUPER BOWL STORY, GAMES I–XXVIII, by Richard J. Brenner. The most spectacular moments in Super Bowl history are brought to life, game by game. 224 pages, including 16 memorable photos. ($4.00/$5.00 Can.)

SHAQUILLE O'NEAL, by Richard J. Brenner. An easy-to-read, photo-filled biography expecially for younger readers. 32 pages. ($3.25/$4.50 Can.)

MICHAEL JORDAN, by Richard J. Brenner. An easy-to-read, photo-filled biography especially for young readers. 32 pages. ($3.50/$4.50 Can.)

WAYNE GRETZKY, by Richard J. Brenner. An easy-to-read, photo-filled biography of hockey's greatest player. 32 pages. Revised edition. ($3.25/$4.50 Can.)

PLEASE SEE NEXT PAGE FOR ORDER FORM

ORDER FORM

Payment must accompany all orders. All payments must be in U.S. dollars.

Postage and handling is $1.35 per book up to a maximum of $6.75. ($1.75 to a maximum of $8.75 in Canada).

Please send me _____ total books as per the following:

☐ BASKETBALL SUPERSTARS ALBUM 1995
☐ SHAQUILLE O'NEAL*LARRY JOHNSON
☐ MICHAEL JORDAN*MAGIC JOHNSON
☐ TROY AIKMAN*STEVE YOUNG
☐ BARRY BONDS*ROBERTO ALOMAR
☐ MARIO LEMIEUX
☐ THE WORLD SERIES, THE GREAT CONTESTS
☐ THE COMPLETE SUPER BOWL STORY, GAMES I–XXVIII
☐ SHAQUILLE O'NEAL
☐ MICHAEL JORDAN
☐ WAYNE GRETZKY

PRICE OF BOOKS $_____
POSTAGE AND HANDLING $_____
TOTAL PAYMENT ENCLOSED $_____

NAME: _____

ADDRESS: _____

CITY: _____ STATE: _____ ZIP CODE: _____

Send to: East End Publishing, Ltd., 54 Alexander Drive, Syosset, NY 11791 USA. Dept. SB28. Allow three weeks for delivery. Discounts are available on orders of 25 or more copies. For details, call (516)364-6383.